D0028874

PRAISE FOR *THE CULTURE CODE*:

'I've been waiting years for someone to write this book – I've built it up in my mind into something extraordinary. But it is even better than I imagined. Daniel Coyle has produced a truly brilliant, mesmerizing read that demystifies the magic of great groups. It blows all other books on culture right out of the water. Read it immediately.' Adam Grant, bestselling author of *Originals*

'If you want to understand how successful groups work – the signals they transmit, the language they speak, the cues that foster creativity – you won't find a more essential guide than *The Culture Code*. This is a marvel of insight and practicality.' Charles Duhigg, bestselling author of *The Power of Habit*

'*The Culture Code* is a step-by-step guidebook to building teams that are not just more effective, but happier. Whether you lead a team or are a team member, this book is a must-read.' Laszlo Bock, CEO of Humu, former SVP of People at Google, and author of *Work Rules!*

CULTURE: from the Latin *cultus*, which means *care*.

Contents

Skill 3 · Establish Purpose   169

For Jen

5 7 9 10 8 6

Random House Business Books
20 Vauxhall Bridge Road
London SW1V 2SA

Random House Business Books is part of the Penguin Random
House group of companies whose addresses can be
found at global.penguinrandomhouse.com.

Penguin
Random House
UK

Copyright © Daniel Coyle 2018

Daniel Coyle has asserted his right to be identified as the
author of this Work in accordance with the Copyright,
Designs and Patents Act 1988.

First published by Random House Business Books in 2018

www.penguin.co.uk

A CIP catalogue record for this book is available
from the British Library.

ISBN 9781847941268

Printed and bound in India by Thomson Press India Ltd.

Penguin Random House is committed to a sustainable future
for our business, our readers and our planet. This book is
made from Forest Stewardship Council® certified paper.

FSC
www.fsc.org
MIX
Paper from
responsible sources
FSC® C018179

The Culture Code

The Secrets of Highly
Successful Groups

Daniel Coyle

BUSINESS
BOOKS

The Culture Code

The Culture Code

When Two Plus Two Equals Ten

Let's start with a question, which might be the oldest question of all: *Why do certain groups add up to be greater than the sum of their parts, while others add up to be less?*

A few years ago the designer and engineer Peter Skillman held a competition to find out. Over several months, he assembled a series of four-person groups at Stanford, the University of California, the University of Tokyo, and several other places. He challenged each group to build the tallest possible structure using the following items:

- twenty pieces of uncooked spaghetti
- one yard of transparent tape
- one yard of string
- one standard-size marshmallow

The contest had one rule: The marshmallow had to end up on top. The fascinating part of the experiment, however, had less to do with the task than with the participants. Some of the teams consisted of business school students. The others consisted of kindergartners.

The business students got right to work. They began talking and thinking strategically. They examined the materials.

They tossed ideas back and forth and asked thoughtful, savvy questions. They generated several options, then honed the most promising ideas. It was professional, rational, and intelligent. The process resulted in a decision to pursue one particular strategy. Then they divided up the tasks and started building.

The kindergartners took a different approach. They did not strategize. They did not analyze or share experiences. They did not ask questions, propose options, or hone ideas. In fact, they barely talked at all. They stood very close to one another. Their interactions were not smooth or organized. They abruptly grabbed materials from one another and started building, following no plan or strategy. When they spoke, they spoke in short bursts: "Here! No, *here!*" Their entire technique might be described as *trying a bunch of stuff together*.

If you had to bet which of the teams would win, it would not be a difficult choice. You would bet on the business school students, because they possess the intelligence, skills, and experience to do a superior job. This is the way we normally think about group performance. We presume skilled individuals will combine to produce skilled performance in the same way we presume two plus two will combine to produce four.

Your bet would be wrong. In dozens of trials, kindergartners built structures that averaged twenty-six inches tall, while business school students built structures that averaged less than ten inches.*

---

* Teams of kindergartners also defeated teams of lawyers (who built towers that averaged fifteen inches) as well as teams of CEOs (twenty-two inches).

The result is hard to absorb because it feels like an illusion. We see smart, experienced business school students, and we find it difficult to imagine that they would combine to produce a poor performance. We see unsophisticated, inexperienced kindergartners, and we find it difficult to imagine that they would combine to produce a successful performance. But this illusion, like every illusion, happens because our instincts have led us to focus on the wrong details. We focus on what we can see—individual skills. But individual skills are not what matters. What matters is the interaction.

The business school students appear to be collaborating, but in fact they are engaged in a process psychologists call status management. They are figuring out where they fit into the larger picture: *Who is in charge? Is it okay to criticize someone's idea? What are the rules here?* Their interactions appear smooth, but their underlying behavior is riddled with inefficiency, hesitation, and subtle competition. Instead of focusing on the task, they are navigating their uncertainty about one another. They spend so much time managing status that they fail to grasp the essence of the problem (the marshmallow is relatively heavy, and the spaghetti is hard to secure). As a result, their first efforts often collapse, and they run out of time.

The actions of the kindergartners appear disorganized on the surface. But when you view them as a single entity, their behavior is efficient and effective. They are not competing for status. They stand shoulder to shoulder and work energetically together. They move quickly, spotting problems and offering help. They experiment, take risks, and notice outcomes, which guides them toward effective solutions.

The kindergartners succeed not because they are smarter but because they work together in a smarter way. They are tapping into a simple and powerful method in which a group of ordinary people can create a performance far beyond the sum of their parts.

This book is the story of how that method works.

Group culture is one of the most powerful forces on the planet. We sense its presence inside successful businesses, championship teams, and thriving families, and we sense when it's absent or toxic. We can measure its impact on the bottom line. (A strong culture increases net income 765 percent over ten years, according to a Harvard study of more than two hundred companies.) Yet the inner workings of culture remain mysterious. We all want strong culture in our organizations, communities, and families. We all know that it works. We just don't know quite *how* it works.

The reason may be based in the way we think about culture. We tend to think about it as a group trait, like DNA. Strong, well-established cultures like those of Google, Disney, and the Navy SEALs feel so singular and distinctive that they seem fixed, somehow predestined. In this way of thinking, culture is a possession determined by fate. Some groups have the gift of strong culture; others don't.

This book takes a different approach. I spent the last four years visiting and researching eight of the world's most successful groups, including a special-ops military unit, an inner-city school, a professional basketball team, a movie studio, a comedy troupe, a gang of jewel thieves, and oth-ers.* I found that their cultures are created by a specific set of skills. These skills, which tap into the power of our social brains to create interactions exactly like the ones used by the kindergartners building the spaghetti tower, form the structure of this book. Skill 1—Build Safety—explores how signals of connection generate bonds of belonging and iden-tity. Skill 2—Share Vulnerability—explains how habits of mutual risk drive trusting cooperation. Skill 3—Establish Purpose—tells how narratives create shared goals and val-ues. The three skills work together from the bottom up, first building group connection and then channeling it into ac-tion. Each part of the book is structured like a tour: We'll first explore how each skill works, and then we'll go into the field to spend time with groups and leaders who use these methods every day. Each part will end with a collection of concrete suggestions on applying these skills to your group.

In the following pages, we'll spend time inside some of the planet's top-performing cultures and see what makes them tick. We'll take a look inside the machinery of the brain and see how trust and belonging are built. Along the way, we'll see that being smart is overrated, that showing fallibility is crucial, and that being nice is not nearly as important as you might think. Above all, we'll see how lead-

---

* I chose groups using the following qualifications: (1) they had performed in the top 1 percent of their domain for at least a decade (where applicable); (2) they had succeeded with a range of different personnel; (3) their culture had been admired by knowledgeable people across their industry and be-yond. To help guard against selection bias, I also looked at many cultures that weren't so successful (see page 40 for an example).

ers of high-performing cultures navigate the challenges of achieving excellence in a fast-changing world. While successful culture can look and feel like magic, the truth is that it's not. Culture is a set of living relationships working toward a shared goal. It's not something you are. It's something you do.

Skill 1

Build Safety

1

The Good Apples

Meet Nick, a handsome, dark-haired man in his twenties seated comfortably in a wood-paneled conference room in Seattle with three other people. To outward appearances, he is an ordinary participant in an ordinary meeting. This appearance, however, is deceiving. The other people in the room do not know it, but his mission is to sabotage the group's performance.

Nick is the key element of an experiment being run by Will Felps, who studies organizational behavior at the University of South Wales in Australia. Felps has brought in Nick to portray three negative archetypes: the Jerk (an aggressive, defiant deviant), the Slacker (a withholder of effort), and the Downer (a depressive Eeyore type). Nick plays these roles inside forty four-person groups tasked with constructing a marketing plan for a start-up. In effect, Felps injects him into the various groups the way a biologist might inject a virus into a body: to see how the system responds. Felps calls it the bad apple experiment.

Nick is really good at being bad. In almost every group, his behavior reduces the quality of the group's performance by 30 to 40 percent. The drop-off is consistent whether he plays the Jerk, the Slacker, or the Downer.

"When Nick is the Downer, everybody comes into the meeting really energized. He acts quiet and tired and at some point puts his head down on his desk," Felps says. "And then as the time goes by, they all start to behave that way, tired and quiet and low energy. By the end, there are three others with their heads down on their desks like him, all with their arms folded."

When Nick plays the Slacker, a similar pattern occurs. "The group quickly picks up on his vibe," Felps says. "They get done with the project very quickly, and they do a half-assed job. What's interesting, though, is that when you ask them about it afterward, they're very positive on the surface. They say, 'We did a good job, we enjoyed it.' But it isn't true. They'd picked up on the attitude that this project really didn't matter, that it wasn't worth their time or energy. I'd gone in expecting that someone in the group would get upset with the Slacker or the Downer. But nobody did. They were like, 'Okay, if that's how it is, then we'll be Slackers and Downers too.'"

Except for one group.

"It's the outlier group," Felps says. "They first came to my attention when Nick mentioned that there was one group that felt really different to him. This group performed well no matter what he did. Nick said it was mostly because of one guy. You can see this guy is causing Nick to get almost infuriated—his negative moves aren't working like they had in the other groups, because this guy could find a way to flip it and engage everyone and get people moving toward the goal."

We'll call this person Jonathan. He is a thin, curly-haired young man with a quiet, steady voice and an easy smile. Despite the bad apple's efforts, Jonathan's group is attentive and energetic, and they produce high-quality results. The more fascinating part, from Felps's view, is that at first glance, Jonathan doesn't seem to be doing anything at all.

"A lot of it is really simple stuff that is almost invisible at first," Felps says. "Nick would start being a jerk, and [Jonathan] would lean forward, use body language, laugh and smile, never in a contemptuous way, but in a way that takes the danger out of the room and defuses the situation. It doesn't seem all that different at first. But when you look more closely, it causes some incredible things to happen."

Over and over Felps examines the video of Jonathan's moves, analyzing them as if they were a tennis serve or a dance step. They follow a pattern: Nick behaves like a jerk, and Jonathan reacts instantly with warmth, deflecting the negativity and making a potentially unstable situation feel solid and safe. Then Jonathan pivots and asks a simple question that draws the others out, and he listens intently and responds. Energy levels increase; people open up and share ideas, building chains of insight and cooperation that move the group swiftly and steadily toward its goal.

"Basically, [Jonathan] makes it safe, then turns to the other people and asks, 'Hey, what do you think of this?'" Felps says. "Sometimes he even asks Nick questions like, 'How would you do that?' Most of all he radiates an idea that is something like, *Hey, this is all really comfortable and engaging, and I'm curious about what everybody else has to say.* It was amazing how such simple, small behaviors kept everybody engaged and on task." Even Nick, almost against his will, found himself being helpful.

The story of the good apples is surprising in two ways. First, we tend to think group performance depends on measurable abilities like intelligence, skill, and experience, not on a subtle pattern of small behaviors. Yet in this case those small behaviors made all the difference.

The second surprise is that Jonathan succeeds without taking any of the actions we normally associate with a strong leader. He doesn't take charge or tell anyone what to do. He doesn't strategize, motivate, or lay out a vision. He doesn't perform so much as create conditions for others to perform, constructing an environment whose key feature is crystal clear: *We are solidly connected.* Jonathan's group succeeds not because its members are smarter but because they are safer.

We don't normally think of safety as being so important. We consider safety to be the equivalent of an emotional weather system—noticeable but hardly a difference maker. But what we see here gives us a window into a powerful idea. Safety is not mere emotional weather but rather the foundation on which strong culture is built. The deeper questions are, *Where does it come from? And how do you go about building it?*

When you ask people inside highly successful groups to describe their relationship with one another, they all tend to choose the same word. This word is not *friends* or *team* or *tribe* or any other equally plausible term. The word they use is *family*. What's more, they tend to describe the feeling of those relationships in the same way.*

"I can't explain it, but things just feel right. I've actually tried to quit a couple times, but I keep coming back to it. There's no feeling like it. These guys are my brothers." (Christopher Baldwin, U.S. Navy's SEAL Team Six)

"It's not rational. Nobody who's purely rational about it does the kinds of things that happen here. There's a teamwork that goes way beyond team and overlaps into the rest of people's lives." (Joe Negron, KIPP charter schools)

"It's a rush, knowing that you can take a huge risk and these people will be there to support you no matter what. We are addicted to that feeling." (Nate Dern, Upright Citizens Brigade comedy troupe)

"We are all about being a familial group, because it allows you to take more risks, give each other permission, and have moments of vulnerability that you could never have in a more normal setting." (Duane Bray, IDEO design)

When I visited these groups, I noticed a distinct pattern of interaction. The pattern was located not in the big things but in little moments of social connection. These interactions were consistent whether the group was a military unit or a movie studio or an inner-city school. I made a list:

* Not coincidentally, many successful groups have adopted the use of family-esque identifiers. People who work at Pixar are Pixarians, and people who work at Google are Googlers. It's the same with Zappos (Zapponians), KIPP (KIPPsters), and others.

- Close physical proximity, often in circles
- Profuse amounts of eye contact
- Physical touch (handshakes, fist bumps, hugs)
- Lots of short, energetic exchanges (no long speeches)
- High levels of mixing; everyone talks to everyone
- Few interruptions
- Lots of questions
- Intensive, active listening
- Humor, laughter
- Small, attentive courtesies (thank-yous, opening doors, etc.)

One more thing: I found that spending time inside these groups was almost physically addictive. I would extend my reporting trips, inventing excuses to stick around for another day or two. I found myself daydreaming about changing occupations so I could apply for a job with them. There was something irresistible about being around these groups that made me crave more connection.

The term we use to describe this kind of interaction is *chemistry*. When you encounter a group with good chemistry, you know it instantly. It's a paradoxical, powerful sensation, a combination of excitement and deep comfort that sparks mysteriously with certain special groups and not with others. There's no way to predict it or control it.

Or is there?

On the third floor of a shiny modernistic building in Cambridge, Massachusetts, a group of scientists is obsessed with understanding the inner workings of group chemistry. The MIT Human Dynamics Lab is a humble set of offices surrounded by a riot of workshops and offices that contain, among other things, a British telephone booth, a mannequin wearing pants made of aluminum foil, and what appears to be a miniature roller coaster suspended from the ceiling. The lab is run by Alex (Sandy) Pentland, a soft-spoken computer science professor with bright eyes, a bushy gray beard, and the easygoing assuredness of a country doctor. Pentland started out his career studying satellite photos of beaver dens, establishing a research method that never really changed: using technology to reveal hidden patterns of behavior.

"Human signaling looks like other animal signaling," Pentland says as we sit down at a coffee table in his small homey office. "You can measure interest levels, who the alpha is, who's cooperating, who's mimicking, who's in synchrony. We have these communication channels, and we do it without thinking about it. For instance, if I lean a few inches closer to you, we might begin mirroring."

Pentland leans closer, raises his bushy eyebrows, and opens his eyes wider. It's a little disconcerting when I find myself doing it too, almost against my will. He smiles reassuringly and leans back. "It only works if we're close enough to physically touch."

Pentland introduces me to a scientist named Oren Lederman, who, as it happens, is in the midst of analyzing a group working on the spaghetti-marshmallow challenge. We walk down the hall to Lederman's office to look at the video. The group consists of three engineers and a lawyer, and their tower is coming together nicely. "This group's performance is probably better than the MBAs but not as good as the kindergartners," Lederman says. "They don't talk as much, which helps."

This is not just Lederman's opinion—it is fact. As we speak, a river of data from the group's performance is rolling across his computer screen, including the percentage of time each person spends talking, the energy levels of their voices, their speaking rates, the smoothness of turn taking, the number of interruptions, and the amount each person's vocal pattern mimics the others. Lederman has captured this data using a small red plastic device the size of a credit card that contains a microphone, GPS, and an array of other sensors.

The device is called a sociometer. It samples the data five times per second and wirelessly streams it to a server, where it is rendered into a series of graphs. These graphs, Pentland informs me, are only the tip of the data iceberg. If they desire, Lederman and Pentland can equip the sociometers to capture proximity and the percentage of time each participant engages in face-to-face contact.

All in all, it is the kind of real-time, deep-dive data that you could imagine being used to measure presidential polling results or a golf swing. But this is a different kind of game. The sociometer captures the proto-language that humans use to form safe connection. This language is made up of belonging cues.

Belonging cues are behaviors that create safe connection in groups. They include, among others, proximity, eye contact, energy, mimicry, turn taking, attention, body language, vocal pitch, consistency of emphasis, and whether everyone talks to everyone else in the group. Like any language, belonging cues can't be reduced to an isolated moment but rather consist of a steady pulse of interactions within a social relationship. Their function is to answer the ancient, ever-present questions glowing in our brains: *Are we safe here? What's our future with these people? Are there dangers lurking?*

"Modern society is an incredibly recent phenomenon," Pentland says. "For hundreds of thousands of years, we needed ways to develop cohesion because we depended so much on each other. We used signals long before we used language, and our unconscious brains are incredibly attuned to certain types of behaviors."

Belonging cues possess three basic qualities:

1. Energy: They invest in the exchange that is occurring
2. Individualization: They treat the person as unique and valued
3. Future orientation: They signal the relationship will continue

These cues add up to a message that can be described with a single phrase: *You are safe here*. They seek to notify our ever-vigilant brains that they can stop worrying about dangers and shift into connection mode, a condition called psychological safety.

"As humans, we are very good at reading cues; we are

incredibly attentive to interpersonal phenomena," says Amy Edmondson, who studies psychological safety at Harvard. "We have a place in our brain that's always worried about what people think of us, especially higher-ups. As far as our brain is concerned, if our social system rejects us, we could die. Given that our sense of danger is so natural and automatic, organizations have to do some pretty special things to overcome that natural trigger."

The key to creating psychological safety, as Pentland and Edmondson emphasize, is to recognize how deeply obsessed our unconscious brains are with it. A mere hint of belonging is not enough; one or two signals are not enough. We are built to require lots of signaling, over and over. This is why a sense of belonging is easy to destroy and hard to build. The dynamic evokes the words of Texas politician Sam Rayburn: "Any jackass can kick down a barn, but it takes a good carpenter to build one."

It's useful to look at the bad apple experiment in this light. Nick was able to disrupt the chemistry of the groups merely by sending a few cues of nonbelonging. His behavior was a powerful signal to the group—*We are not safe*—which immediately caused the group's performance to fall apart. Jonathan, on the other hand, delivered a steady pulse of subtle behaviors that signaled safety. He connected individually, listened intently, and signaled the importance of the relationship. He was a wellspring of belonging cues, and the group responded accordingly.

In recent years, Pentland and his team have used sociometers to capture the interactions of hundreds of groups in post-op wards, call centers, banks, salary negotiations, and business pitch sessions. In each study, they discovered the same pattern: It's possible to predict performance by ignoring all the informational content in the exchange and focusing on a handful of belonging cues.

For example, Pentland and Jared Curhan used sociometers to analyze forty-six simulated negotiations between pairs of business students who played the role of employee and boss. The task was to negotiate the terms for a new position, including salary, company car, vacation, and health benefits. Pentland and Curhan found that the first five minutes of sociometric data strongly predicted the outcomes of the negotiations. In other words, the belonging cues sent in the initial moments of the interaction mattered more than anything they said.

Another experiment analyzed a competition in which entrepreneurs pitched business ideas to a group of executives. Each participant presented their plan to the group; the group then selected and ranked the most promising plans for recommendation to an outside group of angel investors. Pentland found that the sociometers—which tracked only the cues exchanged by presenter and audience and ignored all the informational content—predicted the rankings with nearly perfect accuracy. In other words, the content of the pitch didn't matter as much as the set of cues with which the pitch was delivered and received. (When the angel investors viewed the plans on paper—looking only at informational content and ignoring social signals—they ranked them very differently.)

"The executives [listening to the pitches] thought they were evaluating the plans based on rational measures, such as: How original is this idea? How does it fit the current market? How well developed is this plan?" Pentland wrote. "While listening to the pitches, though, another part of their brain was registering other crucial information, such as: How much does this person believe in this idea? How confident are they when speaking? How determined are they to make this work? And the second set of information— information that the business executives didn't even know they were assessing—is what influenced their choice of business plans to the greatest degree."

"This is a different way of thinking about human beings," Pentland says. "Individuals aren't really individuals. They're more like musicians in a jazz quartet, forming a web of unconscious actions and reactions to complement the others in the group. You don't look at the informational content of the messages; you look at patterns that show how the message is being sent. Those patterns contain many signals that tell us about the relationship and what's really going on beneath the surface."

Overall Pentland's studies show that team performance is driven by five measurable factors:

1. Everyone in the group talks and listens in roughly equal measure, keeping contributions short.
2. Members maintain high levels of eye contact, and their conversations and gestures are energetic.
3. Members communicate directly with one another, not just with the team leader.

4. Members carry on back-channel or side conversations within the team.
5. Members periodically break, go exploring outside the team, and bring information back to share with the others.

These factors ignore every individual skill and attribute we associate with high-performing groups, and replace them with behaviors we would normally consider so primitive as to be trivial. And yet when it comes to predicting team performance, Pentland and his colleagues have calculated nothing is more powerful.

"Collective intelligence is not that different in some ways than apes in a forest," Pentland says. "One [ape] is enthusiastic, and that signal recruits others, and they jump in and start doing stuff together. That's the way group intelligence works, and this is what people don't get. Just hearing something said rarely results in a change in behavior. They're just words. When we see people in our peer group play with an idea, our behavior changes. That's how intelligence is created. That's how culture is created."

They're just words. This is not how we normally think. Normally, we think words matter; we think that group performance correlates with its members' verbal intelligence and their ability to construct and communicate complex ideas. But that assumption is wrong. Words are noise. Group performance depends on behavior that communicates one powerful overarching idea: *We are safe and connected.*

2

The Billion-Dollar Day
When Nothing Happened

In the early 2000s, some of the best minds in America were competing quietly in a race. The goal was to build a software engine that connected Internet user searches with targeted advertisements, an esoteric-sounding task that would potentially unlock a multibillion-dollar market. The question was which company would win.

The overwhelming favorite was Overture, a well-funded Los Angeles outfit led by a brilliant entrepreneur named Bill Gross. Gross had pioneered the field of Internet advertising. He had invented the pay-per-click advertising model, written the code, and built Overture into a thriving business that was generating hundreds of millions of dollars in profits, as well as a recent initial public offering valued at one billion dollars. In other words, the contest between Overture and its competitors appeared to be a profound mismatch. The market had placed a billion-dollar bet on Overture for the same reason that you would have bet on the MBA students to defeat the kindergartners in the spaghetti-marshmallow challenge: because Overture possessed the intelligence, experience, and resources to win.

But Overture did not win. The winner of this race turned

out to be a small, young company called Google. What's more, it's possible to isolate the moment that turned the race in its favor. On May 24, 2002, in Google's kitchen at 2400 Bayshore Parkway in Mountain View, California, Google founder Larry Page pinned a note to the wall. The note contained three words:

THESE ADS SUCK

In the traditional business world, it was not considered normal to leave notes like this in the company kitchen. However, Page was not a traditional businessperson. For starters, he looked like a seventh-grader, with large, watchful eyes, a bowl haircut, and a tendency to speak in abrupt machine-gun bursts. His main leadership technique, if it could be called a technique, consisted of starting and sustaining big, energetic, no-holds-barred debates about how to build the best strategies, products, and ideas. To work at Google was to enter a giant, continuous wrestling match in which no person was considered above the fray.

This approach extended to the raucous all-employee street hockey games in the parking lot ("No one held back when fighting the founders for the puck," recalled one player) and to the all-company Friday forums, where anyone could challenge the founders with any question under the sun, no matter how controversial—and vice versa. Like the hockey games, the Friday forums often turned into collision-filled affairs.

On the day Page pinned his note to the kitchen wall, Google's competition with Overture was not going well.

The project, which Google called the AdWords engine, was struggling to accomplish the basic task of matching search terms to appropriate ads. For example, if you typed in a search for a Kawasaki H1B motorcycle, you'd receive ads from lawyers offering help with your H-1B foreign visa application—precisely the kinds of failures that could doom the project. So Page printed out examples of these failures, scrawled his three-word verdict in capital letters, and pinned the whole mess to the kitchen bulletin board. Then he left.

Jeff Dean was one of the last people in Google's office to see Page's note. A quiet, skinny engineer from Minnesota, Dean was in most ways Page's opposite: smiley, sociable, unfailingly polite, and known around the office for his love of cappuccinos. Dean had no immediate motive to care about the AdWords problem. He worked in Search, which was a different area of the company, and he was more than busy navigating his own urgent problems. But at some point that Friday afternoon, Dean walked over to the kitchen to make a cappuccino and spotted Page's note. He flipped through the attached pages—and as he did, a thought flickered through his mind, a hazy memory of a similar problem he'd encountered a while back.

Dean walked back to his desk and started trying to fix the AdWords engine. He did not ask permission or tell anyone; he simply dove in. On almost every level, his decision made no sense. He was ignoring the mountain of work on his desk in order to wrestle with a difficult problem that no one expected him to take on. He could have quit at any point, and no one would have known. But he did not quit. In fact, he came in on Saturday and worked on the AdWords problem for several hours. On Sunday night, he had dinner with his family and put his two young children to bed. Around nine P.M., he drove back to the office, made another cappuccino, and worked through the night. At 5:05 A.M. on Monday, he sent out an email outlining a proposed fix. Then he drove home, climbed into bed, and went to sleep.

It worked. Dean's fix unlocked the problem, instantly boosting the engine's accuracy scores by double digits. On the strength of that improvement and subsequent others it inspired, AdWords swiftly came to dominate the pay-per-click market. Overture's effort, hamstrung by infighting and bureaucracy, faltered. In the year following Dean's fix, Google's profits went from $6 million to $99 million. By 2014, the AdWords engine was producing $160 million per day, and advertising was providing 90 percent of Google's revenues. The success of the AdWords engine, author Stephen Levy wrote, was "sudden, transforming, decisive, and, for Google's investors and employees, glorious. . . . It became the lifeblood of Google, funding every new idea and innovation the company conceived of thereafter."

Yet that was not the strange part of the story. Because inside Google, there remained one key person for whom this incident didn't mean much—for whom the events of that historic weekend registered so faintly that he barely remembered it. That person happened to be Jeff Dean.

One day in 2013, Google adviser Jonathan Rosenberg approached Dean for a book he was co-writing about Google. Rosenberg wanted to get Dean's version of the story, so he started in—*I want to talk to you about the AdWords engine, Larry's note, the kitchen*—naturally expecting Dean to pick up on the cue and launch into a reminiscence. But Dean didn't do that. Instead, he just stared at Rosenberg with a pleasantly blank expression. Rosenberg, slightly confused, kept going, filling in detail after detail. Only then did Dean's face dawn with the light of recognition—*oh yeah!*

This is not the response you would expect Dean to have. It is roughly the equivalent of Michael Jordan forgetting that he won six NBA titles. But that was how Dean felt and how he still feels today.

"I mean, I remember that it happened," Dean told me. "But to be completely honest, it didn't register strongly in my memory because it didn't feel like that big of a deal. It didn't feel special or different. It was normal. That kind of thing happened all the time."

It was normal. Google personnel were interacting exactly as the kindergartners in the spaghetti-marshmallow challenge interacted. They did not manage their status or worry about who was in charge. Their small building produced high levels of proximity and face-to-face interaction. Page's technique of igniting whole-group debates around solving tough problems sent a powerful signal of identity and connection, as did the no-holds-barred hockey games and wide-open Friday forums. (*Everyone in the group talks and listens in roughly equal measure.*) They communicated in short, direct bursts. (*Members face one another, and their conversations and gestures are energetic.*) Google was a hothouse of belonging cues; its people worked shoulder to shoulder and safely connected, immersed in their projects. Overture, despite its head start and their billion-dollar war chest, was handicapped by bureaucracy. Decision making involved innumerable meetings and discussions about technical, tactical, and strategic matters; everything had to be approved by multiple committees. Overture's belonging scores would likely have been low. "It was a clusterfuck," one employee told *Wired* magazine. Google didn't win because it was smarter. It won because it was safer. *

Let's take a closer look at how belonging cues function in your brain. Say I give you a moderately tricky puzzle where the goal is to arrange colors and shapes on a map. You can work on it as long as you like. After explaining the task, I leave you to your work. Two minutes later I pop back in and hand you a slip of paper with a handwritten note. I tell you that the note is from a fellow participant named Steve, whom you've never met. "Steve did the puzzle earlier and wanted to share a tip with you," I say. You read the tip and get back to work. And that's when everything changes.

Without trying, you start working harder on the puzzle. Areas deep in your brain begin to light up. You are more motivated—twice as much. You work more than 50 percent

---

* The Google/Overture pattern is not unique to them. In the 1990s, sociologists James Baron and Michael Hannan analyzed the founding cultures of nearly two hundred technology start-ups in Silicon Valley. They found that most followed one of three basic models: the star model, the professional model, and the commitment model. The star model focused on finding and hiring the brightest people. The professional model focused on building the group around specific skill sets. The commitment model, on the other hand, focused on developing a group with shared values and strong emotional bonds. Of these, the commitment model consistently led to the highest rates of success. During the tech-bubble burst of 2000, the start-ups that used the commitment model survived at a vastly higher rate than the other two models, and achieved initial public offerings three times more often.

longer, with significantly more energy and enjoyment. What's more, the glow endures. Two weeks later, you are inclined to take on similar challenges. In essence, that slip of paper changes you into a smarter, more attuned version of yourself.

Here's the thing: Steve's tip was not actually useful. It contained zero relevant information. All the changes in motivation and behavior you experienced afterward were due to the signal that you were connected to someone who cared about you.

We get another example of how belonging cues work in an experiment that might be called Would You Give a Stranger Your Phone? It consists of two scenarios and a question.

> SCENARIO 1: You are standing in the rain at a train station. A stranger approaches and politely says, "Can I borrow your cellphone?"
> SCENARIO 2: You are standing in the rain at a train station. A stranger approaches and politely says, "I'm so sorry about the rain. Can I borrow your cellphone?"
> QUESTION: To which stranger are you more likely to respond?

At first glance, there's not a lot of difference between the two scenarios. Both strangers are making an identical request that involves a significant leap of trust. Besides, the more important factor here would seem to have less to do with them than with *you*; namely your natural disposition toward handing a valuable possession to a stranger. All in all, a reasonable person might predict that the two approaches would yield roughly equal response rates.

A reasonable person would be wrong. When Alison Wood Brooks of Harvard Business School performed the experiment, she discovered that the second scenario caused the response rate to jump 422 percent. Those six words—*I'm so sorry about the rain*—transformed people's behavior. They functioned exactly the way Steve's tip did in the puzzle experiment. They were an unmistakable signal: *This is a safe place to connect.* You hand over your cellphone—and create a connection—without thinking.

"These are massive effects," says Dr. Gregory Walton of Stanford, who performed the Steve's tip experiment and others. "These are little cues that signal a relationship, and they totally transform the way people relate, how they feel, and how they behave."*

One of his most vivid examples of the power of belonging cues is a study by an Australian group that examined 772 patients who had been admitted to the hospital after a suicide attempt. In the months after their release, half received a series of postcards that read as follows:

---

* Here's a handy use of this effect: Thinking about your ancestors makes you smarter. A research team led by Peter Fischer found that spending a few minutes contemplating your family tree (as opposed to contemplating a friend, or a shopping list, or nothing at all) significantly boosted performance on tests of cognitive intelligence. Their hypothesis is that thinking about our connections to the group increases our feelings of autonomy and control.

Dear _____

It has been a short time since you were here at New-castle Mater Hospital, and we hope things are going well for you. If you wish to drop us a note, we would be happy to hear from you.

Best wishes,
[signature]

Over the next two years, members of the group that received the postcards were readmitted at half the rate of the control group.

"A small signal can have a huge effect," Walton says. "But the deeper thing to realize is that you can't just give a cue once. This is all about establishing relationships, conveying the fact that I'm interested in you, and that all the work we do together is in the context of that relationship. It's a narrative—you have to keep it going. It's not unlike a romantic relationship. How often do you tell your partner that you love them? It may be true, but it's still important to let them know, over and over."

This idea—that belonging needs to be continually refreshed and reinforced—is worth dwelling on for a moment. If our brains processed safety logically, we would not need this steady reminding. But our brains did not emerge from millions of years of natural selection because they process safety logically. They emerged because they are obsessively on the lookout for danger.

This obsession originates in a structure deep in the core of the brain. It's called the amygdala, and it's our primeval vigilance device, constantly scanning the environment. When we sense a threat, the amygdala pulls our alarm cord, setting off the fight-or-flight response that floods our body with stimulating hormones, and it shrinks our perceived world to a single question: *What do I need to do to survive?*

Science has recently discovered, however, that the amygdala isn't just about responding to danger—it also plays a vital role in building social connections. It works like this: When you receive a belonging cue, the amygdala switches roles and starts to use its immense unconscious neural horsepower to build and sustain your social bonds. It tracks members of your group, tunes in to their interactions, and sets the stage for meaningful engagement. In a heartbeat, it transforms from a growling guard dog into an energetic guide dog with a single-minded goal: to make sure you stay tightly connected with your people.

On brain scans, this moment is vivid and unmistakable, as the amygdala lights up in an entirely different way. "The whole thing flips," says Jay Van Bavel, social neuroscientist at New York University. "The moment you're part of a group, the amygdala tunes in to who's in that group and starts intensely tracking them. Because these people are valuable to you. They were strangers before, but they're on your team now, and that changes the whole dynamic. It's such a powerful switch—it's a big top-down change, a total reconfiguration of the entire motivational and decision-making system."

All this helps reveal a paradox about the way belonging works. Belonging feels like it happens from the inside out, but in fact it happens from the outside in. Our social brains light up when they receive a steady accumulation of almost-invisible cues: *We are close, we are safe, we share a future.*

Here, then, is a model for understanding how belonging works: as a flame that needs to be continually fed by signals of safe connection. When Larry Page and Jeff Dean participated in the whole-company challenges, the anything-goes meetings, and the raucous hockey games, they were feeding that flame. When Jonathan protected the bad apple group from Nick's negative behavior, he was feeding that flame. When a stranger apologizes for the rain before asking to borrow your cellphone, she is feeding that flame. Cohesion happens not when members of a group are smarter but when they are lit up by clear, steady signals of safe connection.

This model helps us approach belonging less as a mystery of fate than as a process that can be understood and controlled. A good way to explore this process is by examining three situations where belonging formed despite overwhelming odds. The first involves soldiers in Flanders during the winter of 1914. The second involves office workers in Bangalore, India. The third involves what might be the worst culture on the planet.

3
The Christmas Truce, the One-Hour Experiment, and the Missileers

The Christmas Truce

Of all the difficult and dangerous battlefields in history, the Flanders trenches during the winter of 1914 might top the list. Military scholars tell us that this is due to the fact that World War I marked the historical intersection of modern weapons and medieval strategy. But in truth, it was mostly due to the mud. The Flanders trenches were located below sea level, dug out of greasy clay so waterlogged that a rainstorm could transform them into canals. They were cold and miserable, an ideal breeding ground for rats, fleas, disease, and all manner of pestilence.

The worst part, however, was the closeness of the enemy. Opposing troops were only a few hundred feet apart in many points and occasionally much less. (At one place near Vimy Ridge, two observation posts stood seven meters apart.) Grenades and artillery were a constant threat; a carelessly lit match was an invitation for a sniper's bullet. As future prime minister Harold Macmillan, then a lieutenant in the Grenadier Guards, wrote, "One can look for miles and see no human being. But in those miles of country lurk . . . it seems thousands, even hundreds of thousands of men, planning against each other perpetually some new device of death. Never showing themselves, they launch at each other bullet, bomb, aerial torpedo and shell."

Beneath the mud resided deeper layers of historical hatred between the Allies and the Germans. English and French newspapers printed fervent myths about how German barbarians were melting down innocent victims to make soap. For their part, German schoolchildren were reciting Ernst Lissauer's "Hymn of Hate," which was only slightly less subtle:

> *You we will hate with a lasting hate,*
> *We will never forgo our hate,*
> *Hate by water and hate by land,*
> *Hate of the head and hate of the hand,*
> *Hate of the hammer and hate of the crown,*
> *Hate of seventy millions choking down.*
> *We love as one, we hate as one,*
> *We have one foe and one alone—*
> *ENGLAND!*

The war began in August. As the weeks and months passed, the two sides systematically killed each other and were killed, the bodies strewn in the barbed wire of no-man's-land. As Christmas approached, voices in distant capitals argued for a temporary cease-fire. In Rome, Pope Benedict appealed for holiday peace; in Washington, D.C., a Senate resolution requested a twenty-day break in the fighting. Military leaders on both sides swiftly deemed this idea impossible and informed their troops to expect surprise attacks on Christmas. Any soldier who attempted to create an illicit truce, they warned, would be court-martialed.

Then on Christmas Eve, something happened. It's difficult to determine precisely where it began, but it appeared to have been spontaneous, occurring independently at several places along the front. It started with songs. Some were Christmas carols; some were military songs. In most places, the singing went back and forth for a while, with each side applauding or jeering the other's renditions.

Then something even stranger happened: The soldiers began to climb out of their trenches and approach each other in a friendly way. Outside a town called La Chapelle d'Armentières, English soldiers heard a German voice call out, in English, "I am a lieutenant! Gentlemen, my life is in your hands, for I am out of my trench and walking toward you. Will one of your officers meet me halfway?"

Rifleman Percy Jones figured it was a surprise attack. As he later wrote:

We commenced polishing up ammunition and rifles and getting all ready for speedy action. In fact we were about to loose off a few rounds at the biggest light when . . . words were heard (probably through a megaphone), "Englishmen, Englishmen. Don't shoot. You don't shoot, we don't shoot." Then followed a remark about Christmas. This was all very well, but we had heard so many yarns about German treachery that we kept a very sharp lookout.

How it happened I don't know, but shortly after

this our boys had lights out and the enemy troops were busy singing each other's songs, punctuated with terrific salvos of applause. The scene from my sentry post was hardly creditable. Straight ahead were three large lights, with figures perfectly visible around them. The German trenches . . . were illuminated with hundreds of little lights. Far away to the left, where our lines bent, a few lights showed our A Company trenches, where the men were thundering out "My Little Grey Home in the West." At the conclusion . . . the Saxons burst into loud cheers and obliged with some German tune. They also sang one of their national airs to the tune of "God Save the King." We replied with the Austrian hymn, at which the applause was terrific.

Back at British High Command, Field Marshal Sir John French received puzzling reports that unarmed German soldiers were "running from the German trenches across to ours, holding Christmas trees above their heads." French issued immediate orders to "prevent any recurrence of such conduct, and called the local commanders to strict account." His orders had no effect. The truce grew. The soldiers involved seemed to have no more idea why this was happening than Sir John French did. They saw it happen and participated in it, and it still felt utterly inexplicable. Diarists on both sides would refer to the surreality of the event, many describing it as kind of a waking dream.

For many years, historians assumed that the story of the Christmas Truce was exaggerated, an isolated instance that had been inflated by softheaded newspaper writers. But as they dug deeper, they found the opposite was true. The truce was far bigger than had been reported, involving tens of thousands of men along two-thirds of the British-held line. The interactions included eating, drinking, cooking, singing, playing soccer matches, exchanging photos, bartering, and burying the dead.* In the annals of history, there are few cases where all-out violence pivoted so swiftly and completely to familial warmth. The deeper question is how it happened.

The traditional way of explaining the Christmas Truce is to see it as a story about how the shared meaning of the holiday can awaken the better angels of our nature. This way of thinking is attractive, but it fails to explain what actually occurred. There were plenty of other battlefields throughout history where enemies experienced shared spiritual holidays, yet did not engage in anything remotely approaching this level of connection.

The picture shifts, however, if we look at it through the lens of belonging cues. One of the most detailed accounts can be found in *Trench Warfare 1914–1918* by Tony Ashworth. Over the course of 288 pages, Ashworth provides the historical equivalent of a slow-motion replay of the forces that triggered the Christmas Truce. He shows that it began not on Christmas but weeks before, when a steady flow of interactions created bonds of safety, identity, and trust. Ash-

---

* One soldier who didn't appreciate the truce was German corporal Adolf Hitler, who was in reserve near the Flanders front. "Such a thing should not happen in wartime," he is alleged to have said to his fellow soldiers who joined in. "Have you no German sense of honor left at all?"

worth likens the arrival of the Christmas Truce to "the sudden surfacing of the whole of an iceberg, visible to all including non-combatants, which for most of the war remained largely submerged."

Ashworth details the physical closeness of the two sides. While the closeness brought violence, it also brought connection, through the smells of cooking and the sounds of voices, laughter, and songs. Soldiers on both sides became aware that they followed the same daily rhythms and routines of meals, resupply, and troop rotations. Both sides dealt with the combination of numbing routine and raw terror that made up military life. Both sides hated the cold and wet; both sides longed for home. As Ashworth puts it, "The process of mutual empathy among antagonists was facilitated by their proximity in trench war, and, further, was reinforced as the assumptions made by each of the other's likely actions were confirmed by subsequent events. Moreover, by getting to know the 'neighbor' in the trench opposite, each adversary realized that the other endured the same stress, reacted in the same way, and thus was not so very different from himself."

Microtruces began in early November. The British and Germans had a habit of delivering rations to the trenches around the same time. While the troops ate, the shooting would stop. The next day the same thing happened at precisely the same time. And the next day. And the next. From meals, the microtruces spread to other behaviors. When heavy rainfall made movement difficult, both sides would stop fighting. On cold nights in some sectors, troops from both sides would venture forth to gather dry straw for bedding, and both would withhold fire so they could work in peace. The tacit cease-fires grew to include supply lines (off limits), latrines (same), and the gathering of casualties after a battle.

Those interactions sound casual, but in fact each involves an emotional exchange of unmistakable clarity. One side stops shooting, leaving itself exposed. The other side senses that exposure but does nothing. Each time it happens, both experience the relief and gratitude of safe connection—*they saw me.*

The connections grew. In several sectors, certain areas were designated as "out of bounds" for sniper fire and designated with white flags. One English artillery unit spoke of its "pet sniper" on the German side who would send his "good night kiss" every night promptly at nine-fifteen P.M., then shoot no more until the following morning. In another sector, an English machine-gunner would shoot out the rhythm of a popular song called "Policeman's Holiday," and his German counterpart would provide an answering refrain. The trenches became a petri dish of belonging cues. Each cue, by itself, would not have had much of an impact. But together, repeated day after day, they combined to create conditions that set the stage for a deeper connection.

In the soldiers' accounts, it's possible to see these connections strengthen. One morning after a violent battle at the end of November, Edward Hulse, a captain in the Second Scots Guard, wrote about an impromptu moment of empathy.

The morning after the attack, there was an almost tacit
understanding as to no firing, and about 6:15 A.M.
I saw eight or nine German shoulders and heads appear, and then three crawled out a few feet in front
of their parapet and began dragging in some of our
fellows who were either dead or unconscious. . . .
I passed down the order that none of my men were to
fire and this seems to have been done all down the
line. I helped one of the men in myself, and was not
fired on, at all.

That incident seems to have affected Hulse. Several weeks
later, from a post behind the lines, he hatched a plan. He
wrote:

We return to the trenches tomorrow, and shall be in
them on Christmas Day. Germans or no Germans . . .
we are going to have a 'ell of a bust, including plum
puddings for the whole battalion. I have got a select
little party together, who, led by my stentorian voice,
are going to take up a position in our trenches where
we are closest to the enemy, about 80 yards, and from
10 P.M. onwards we are going to give the enemy every
conceivable form of song in harmony, from carols to
Tipperary. . . . My fellows are most amused with the
idea, and will make a rare noise when we get at it.
Our object will be to drown the now far too familiar
strains of "Deutschland über Alles" and the "Wacht
am Rhein" we hear from their trenches every evening.

The Germans responded with their own barrage of songs. Some were similar, and the Latin songs were identical. From a psychological perspective, they conveyed a meaning that both sides understood, a shared burst of belief and identity.

Hulse walked out and met his counterpart, a German major. The Germans helped the English bury their dead, and the German commander handed Hulse a medal and some letters belonging to an English captain who had died and fallen into the German trench a week earlier. Overcome with emotion, Hulse took off his silk scarf and handed it to the German. "It was absolutely astounding," he later wrote, "and if I had seen it on a cinematograph film I should have sworn that it was faked!"

A few miles away, near Ploegsteert Wood, Corporal John Ferguson crouched in his trench, trying to figure out what was happening. He later wrote:

We shouted back and forward until Old Fritz [the German officer] clambered out of the trench, and accompanied by three others of my section, we went out to meet him. . . . "Make for the light," he called and as we came nearer we saw he had his flash lamp in his hand, putting it in and out to guide us.

We shook hands, wishing each other a Merry Xmas, and were soon conversing as if we had known each other for years. We were in front of their wire entanglements and surrounded by Germans—Fritz and I in the centre talking, and Fritz occasionally translating to his friends what I was saying. We stood inside the circle like street-corner orators. . . . Where they couldn't talk the language they were making themselves understood by signs, and everyone seemed to be getting along nicely. Here we were laughing and chatting to men whom only a few hours before we were trying to kill!

Hulse and Ferguson, like so many others, were astounded. But it was not really astounding. At the point when the English and the Germans stepped out onto that field, they had already been in conversation for a long time, both sides sending volleys of belonging cues that lit up their amygdalas with a simple message: *We are the same. We are safe. I'll go halfway if you will.* And so they did.*

The One-Hour Experiment

If you had to pick an environment that is the opposite of the Flanders trenches, you might pick the WIPRO call center in Bangalore, India. WIPRO is the model of a successful call center. It is organized. It is highly efficient. The days consist of the same work that happens in call centers all over the world: A caller phones in with issues about a device or a service, and WIPRO's agents attempt to remedy it. WIPRO

---

* The final chapter of this story is less inspiring but equally informative. The generals on both sides, on learning of the truce, put a stop to it with relative ease. They ordered raids, rotated troops to stop fraternization, and swiftly destroyed the foundation of belonging that had been so incrementally built. The following Christmas both sides fought as usual.

(pronounced WHIP-row) is by almost every measure a nice place to work. It features competitive salaries and high-quality facilities. The company treats employees well, providing good food, transportation, and social activities. But in the late 2000s, WIPRO found itself facing a persistent problem: Its employees were leaving in droves, as many as 50 to 70 percent each year. They left for the usual reasons—they were young or taking a different job—and for reasons they couldn't quite articulate. At bottom, they lacked a strong connection to the group.

WIPRO's leaders initially tried to fix things by increasing incentives. They boosted salaries, added perks, and touted their company's award as one of India's best employers. All these moves made sense—but none of them helped. Employees kept leaving at precisely the same rate as before. And so in the fall of 2010, with the help of researchers Bradley Staats, Francesco Gino, and Daniel Cable, they decided to embark on a small experiment.

The experiment went like this: Several hundred new hires were divided into two groups, plus the usual control group. Group one received standard training plus an additional hour that focused on WIPRO's identity. These trainees heard about the company's successes, met a "star performer," and answered questions about their first impressions of WIPRO. At the end of the hour, they received a fleece sweatshirt embroidered with the company's name.

Group two also received the standard training, plus an additional hour focused not on the company but on the employee. These trainees were asked questions like *What is unique about you that leads to your happiest times and best performances at work?* In a brief exercise, they were asked to imagine they were lost at sea and to consider what special skills they might bring to the situation. At the end of the hour, they were given a fleece sweatshirt embroidered with their name alongside the company's name.

Staats didn't expect the experiment to show much. High attrition is the norm in the call center world, and WIPRO's attrition rates were firmly in line with industry averages. And besides, Staats wasn't inclined to believe a one-hour intervention could make a long-term impact. A former engineer who spent the first years of his career as an analyst at Goldman Sachs, he isn't some pie-in-the-sky academic. He knows how things work in the real world.

"I was pretty sure that our experiment was going to show a small effect, if any at all," Staats says. "I saw the onboarding process in rational, transactional, informational terms. You show up at a new job on the first day, and there's a straightforward process where you learn how to act, how to behave, and that's all there is to it."

Seven months later the numbers came in, and Staats was, as he puts it, "completely shocked." Trainees from group two were 250 percent more likely than those from group one and 157 percent more likely than those from the control group to still be working at WIPRO. The hour of training had transformed group two's relationship with the company. They went from being noncommittal to being engaged on a far deeper level. The question was why.

The answer is belonging cues. The trainees in group one received zero signals that reduced the interpersonal distance between themselves and WIPRO. They received lots of information about WIPRO and star performers, plus a nice company sweatshirt, but nothing that altered that fundamental distance.

The group two trainees, on the other hand, received a steady stream of individualized, future-oriented, amygdala-activating belonging cues. All these signals were small—a personal question about their best times at work, an exercise that revealed their individual skills, a sweatshirt embroidered with their name. These signals didn't take much time to deliver, but they made a huge difference because they created a foundation of psychological safety that built connection and identity.

"My old way of thinking about this issue was wrong," Staats says. "It turns out that there are a whole bunch of effects that take place when we are pleased to be a part of a group, when we are part of creating an authentic structure for us to be more ourselves. All sorts of beneficial things play out from those first interactions."

I talked with Dilip Kumar, one of the original WIPRO trainees who had taken part in the experiment. I expected him to share vivid memories of the session, but talking to him about his orientation was a lot like talking to Jeff Dean about fixing the AdWords engine: His sense of belonging was so strong that he'd basically forgotten that the experiment had ever happened. "To be honest, I don't remember much about that day, but I remember it felt motivating," said Kumar. He laughed. "I guess it must have worked, because I am still here, and I definitely like it."

The Opposite of Belonging

While it's useful to spend time with successful cultures, it's equally useful to travel to the other end of the spectrum, to examine cultures that fail. The most instructive may be those where the group fails with such consistency that it approaches a kind of perfection. This is where we find the story of the Minuteman missileers.

The Minuteman missileers are the 750 or so men and women who work as nuclear missile launch officers. They are stationed at remote air force bases in Wyoming, Montana, and North Dakota, and their job, for which they are extensively trained, is to control some of the most powerful weapons on earth, 450 Minuteman III missiles. The missiles are sixty feet tall, weigh 80,000 pounds, and can travel 15,000 miles per hour to any spot on the globe within thirty minutes, each delivering twenty times more explosive energy than the Hiroshima bomb.

The missileers are part of a system designed in the late 1940s by General Curtis LeMay, a larger-than-life figure whose mission was to make the American nuclear force a perfectly functioning machine. "Every man a coupling or tube; every organization a rampart of transistors, battery of condensers," LeMay wrote. "All rubbed up, no corrosion. Alert." LeMay was called "The Toughest Cop of the Western World" by *Life* magazine, and his confidence was unbounded. One time he stepped into a bomber with a lit cigar. When a crew member warned him that the bomber might explode, LeMay replied, "It wouldn't dare."

LeMay's system worked well enough for several decades.

But in recent years failures began to occur with increasing regularity:

- August 2007: Crews at Minot Air Force Base mistakenly loaded six nuclear-tipped cruise missiles onto a B-52 bomber, flew them to Barksdale Air Force Base in Louisiana, and allowed them to sit unattended on a runway for several hours.

- December 2007: Minot's missile launch crews failed the subsequent inspection. Inspectors noted that at the time of the visit some of Minot's security personnel were playing video games on their cellphones.

- 2008: A Pentagon report noted "a dramatic and unacceptable decline" in the air force's commitment to the nuclear mission. One Pentagon official was quoted as saying, "It makes the hair stand up on the back of my neck."

- 2009: Thirty tons of solid rocket boosters ended up in a ditch near Minot when the tractor-trailer carrying them drove off the road.

- 2012: A federally funded study revealed high levels of burnout, frustration, aggravation, and spousal abuse in the missileer force, and it showed that court-martial rates in the nuclear missile force were more than twice as high as in the rest of the air force. As one missileer told researchers, "We don't care if things go properly. We just don't want to get into trouble."

- 2013: Missile officers at Minot Air Force Base received a "marginal" rating—the equivalent of a D grade—when three of the eleven crews were rated "unqualified." Nineteen officers were removed from launch duty and forced to retake proficiency tests. Lieutenant General James Kowalski, commander of the nuclear forces, says that the greatest nuclear threat to America "is an accident. The greatest risk to my force is doing something stupid."

- 2014: Minuteman maintenance crews caused an accident involving a nuclear-armed missile in its silo.

Every time a failure occurred, commanders responded by cracking down. As General Kowalski put it, "This is not a training problem. This is some people out there having a problem with discipline." After the string of incidents in the spring of 2013, Lieutenant Colonel Jay Folds wrote to the combat crew at Minot that they had "fallen . . . and it's time to stand ourselves back up." He described "rot in the crew force" and the need to "crush any rules violators." "We need to hit the reset button and restructure the crew force to take you out of your comfort zones (which are rotten comfort zones) and rebuild from the ground up," Folds wrote. "Turn the TVs off and work hard on your proficiency. . . . You better bring your A-game every day. You must be ready, on a moment's notice, for any eval, any test, any field visit, any certification, etc. Gone is the academic environment of the past (or the environment where we handed things to you on a silver platter because we thought that's the way you take care of the crew force). . . . Bring to my attention immediately any officer who badmouths a senior officer, or badmouths the new culture we're trying to reconstruct. There will be consequences!"

From afar, it looked like an impressive, all-hands-on-deck, get-tough response. The problem was, none of it worked. The mistakes kept happening. A few months after the Folds manifesto, Major General Michael Carey, who was responsible for overseeing the nation's intercontinental ballistic missiles, was fired for misconduct during an official trip to Moscow.* Soon afterward an air force investigation at Malmstrom Air Force Base implicated two missileers on charges of illegal possession, use, and distribution of cocaine, ecstasy, and bath salts. When investigators examined the cellphones of the accused officers, they uncovered an elaborate system for cheating on proficiency tests, sparking another investigation that ended up implicating thirty-four of Malmstrom's missileers, plus sixty more who knew about the cheating and failed to report it.

Everyone agrees that missileer culture is broken. The deeper question is why. If you think about culture as an extension of a group's character—its DNA—you tend to see

---

* Here is an excerpt from the forty-two-page air force report on Carey's misconduct: "[Carey] appeared drunk and, in the public area [of the Zurich airport], talked loudly about the importance of his position as commander of the only operational nuclear force in the world and that he saves the world from war every day." In Moscow, he drank heavily and during a monastery tour attempted to fist-bump his Russian tour guide. He repeatedly interrupted his hosts during their ceremonial toasts to make his own. He sought out the company of those he called "two hot women" and accompanied them to a bar called La Cantina. According to the report, he kept asking the band to allow him to come onstage to sing and play guitar with them. The report notes, "The band did not allow Maj. Gen. Carey to play with them."

the missileers as lazy, selfish, and lacking in character. This leads to the type of get-tough remedies the air force leadership attempted, and their failure leaves you only to confirm the original assumption: The missileers are lazy, immature, and selfish.

However, if we look at missileer culture through the lens of belonging cues, the picture shifts. Belonging cues have to do not with character or discipline but with building an environment that answers basic questions: *Are we connected? Do we share a future? Are we safe?* Let's take them one by one.

Are we connected? It is hard to conceive of a situation of less physical, social, and emotional connection than that of the missileers. They spend twenty-four-hour rotations paired up in chilly, cramped missile silos with Eisenhower-era technology. "These things have been lived in continuously for forty years," one missileer told me. "They get cleaned but not really. Sewage lines are corroding. Asbestos is everywhere. People hate being there."

Do we share a future? When the silos were built, the missileers were as crucial a part of America's defense as their pilot brethren; receiving a launch order from the president was a real possibility. Serving as a missileer functioned as a stepping-stone for a career in space command, air combat command, and other areas. But the end of the Cold War changed the missileers' future. They are training for a mission that no longer exists. Not surprisingly, career paths out of missiles have dwindled or vanished entirely.

"The writing's on the wall," says Bruce Blair, a former missileer who is now a research scholar at the Program on

Science and Global Security at Princeton. "No one wants to stay in missiles. There's no chance of promotion. You're not going to make general coming through missiles. What's more, the command has shut down some of the options of cross-training out of nuclear into other commands, which has delivered the message that you guys are stuck on the island of misfit toys."

"For the first couple months it's kind of exciting," another former missileer told me. "But the shine starts to come off pretty quickly. You do it over and over again. You realize, this is not going to change, this is never going to change."

Are we safe? The biggest risk in the missileer's world is not the missiles but the constant barrage of proficiency, certification, and nuclear-readiness tests, each of which requires near-perfection and each of which might scuttle their career. These tests often involve memorizing a five-inch-thick binder filled with two-sided sheets of launch codes. Missileers must score 100 percent on certain portions of the tests, or else they fail.

"The checklists are impossibly long and detailed, bizarrely rigid and strict. It's basically inhuman," Blair says. "You're either perfect or you're a bum. The result is that when you get out of the spotlight of the authority and travel to a remote underground launch control center with one other person, you close that eight-ton blast door behind you. All the standards get dropped, and you start taking shortcuts."

As one missileer told me, "Every deviation is treated as if it's violating a presidential launch order. Make a critical error? You're done. You're the shitty guy. There is no such thing as doing an outstanding job. You either do it right, or you get punished. If you admit a mistake or ask for help, you ruin your reputation. Everyone walks around like scared puppies. So you get a feedback loop. Something bad happens, everybody screams and yells, then they institute more evaluations, which makes everybody more demoralized, more tired, so you make more mistakes."

It all adds up to a perfectly designed storm of antibelonging cues, where there is no connection, no future, and no safety. Seen in this way, missileer culture is not a result of an internal lack of discipline and character but of an environment custom-built to destroy cohesion. Indeed, the former launch officers I spoke with were smart, eloquent, thoughtful people who seemed to have found successful and fulfilling lives once they left the broken missileer culture. The difference wasn't in the content of their character. It was in the lack of safety and belonging in their culture.

It's useful to contrast the missileers' dysfunctional culture with that of their navy counterparts who work in nuclear submarines. At first glance, the two groups seem roughly similar: Both spend vast amounts of time isolated from the rest of society, both are tasked with memorizing and executing tedious protocols, and both are oriented toward Cold War nuclear deterrence missions whose time has passed. Where they differ, however, is in the density of the belonging cues in their respective environments. Sailors in submarines have close physical proximity, take part in purposeful activity (global patrols that include missions beyond deterrence), and are part of a career pathway that can lead to the highest positions in the navy. Perhaps as a result, the nuclear submarine fleet has thus far mostly avoided the kinds of problems that plague the missileers, and in many cases have developed high-performing cultures.

So far we've explored the process for creating belonging. Now we'll turn to the more practical question of applying this process in the real world. We'll do this by meeting two leaders who build belonging in their groups using vastly different but equally effective methods. First, a basketball coach will give us an up-close insight into the skill of building relationships. Then an unconventional retail billionaire will explain how he creates belonging at a higher level through systems and design.

4

How to Build Belonging

The Relationship Maker

A while back a writer named Neil Paine set out to determine who was the best National Basketball Association coach of the modern era. He devised an algorithm that used player performance metrics to predict how many games a team should win. He crunched numbers for every NBA coach since 1979 in order to measure "wins above expectation"— that is, the number of times a coach's team won a game that, measured by their players' skills, they had no business winning. He then plotted the results on a graph.

For the most part, Paine's graph portrays an orderly and predictable world. The vast majority of coaches win roughly the number of games they should win, given their players' abilities—except for one. His name is Gregg Popovich. Coach of the San Antonio Spurs, he resides alone at the far reaches of the graph, a planet unto himself. Under his leadership, the Spurs have won no fewer than 117 games more than they should have, a rate more than double that of the next-nearest coach. This is why the Spurs rank as the most successful team in American sports over the last two decades, winning five championships and a higher percentage of games than the New England Patriots, the St. Louis Cardinals, or any other storied franchise. The title of Paine's graph is "Gregg Popovich Is Impossible."

It's not hard to figure out why Popovich's teams win, because the evidence is in plain view on the court. The Spurs consistently perform the thousand little unselfish behaviors— the extra pass, the alert defense, the tireless hustle—that puts the team's interest above their own.* "Selfless," LeBron James said. "Guys move, cut, pass, you've got a shot, you take it. But it's all for the team and it's never about the individual." Playing against them, said Marcin Gortat of the Washington Wizards, "was like listening to Mozart." What's hard to figure out is how Popovich does it.

Popovich, sixty-eight, is a hard-core, old-school, unapologetic authoritarian, a steel-spined product of the Air Force Academy who values discipline above all. His disposition has been compared to that of a dyspeptic bulldog, and he possesses a temper that could be described as "volcanic," with much of the lava being funneled at his star players. Some of his more memorable eruptions are collected on YouTube, under titles such as "Popovich Yells and Destroys Thiago Splitter," "Popovich Tells Danny Green to Shut the

---

* This is more impressive when you consider that selfishness is incentivized in the NBA. In 2013, researchers Eric Uhlmann and Christopher Barnes analyzed nine seasons worth of NBA games, comparing behavior in the regular season with behavior in the play-offs. They discovered that players who made a shot in the play-offs received $22,044.55 additional salary per field goal made. Players who passed the ball to a teammate who made a shot lost $6,116.69. Passing the ball instead of shooting is the equivalent of handing a teammate $28,161.24.

F— Up," and "Popovich Furious at Tony Parker." In short, he embodies a riddle: How does a cranky, demanding coach create the most cohesive team in all of sports?

One common answer is that the Spurs are smart about drafting and developing unselfish, hardworking, team-oriented individuals. This is a tempting explanation, because the Spurs clearly make a concerted effort to select high-character individuals. (Their scouting template includes a check box labeled "Not a Spur." A check in this box means the player will not be pursued, no matter how talented he is.)

But on closer examination, this explanation doesn't add up. Many other NBA teams make similar efforts to identify, select, and develop hardworking, team-oriented, high-character individuals. And besides, a significant number of Spurs do not exactly fit the Eagle Scout profile. When Boris Diaw played for Charlotte, for instance, he was criticized for being lazy, party-oriented, and overweight; Patty Mills was released by his Chinese team for allegedly faking a hamstring injury; and Danny Green was cut by Cleveland, in part, for his casual approach to team defense.

So the Spurs are not simply selecting unselfish players or forcing them to play this way. Something is making their players—even those who were selfish elsewhere—behave unselfishly when they put on a Spurs jersey. The question is what that something is.

It's the morning of April 4, 2014, and the mood in the San Antonio practice facility is tense. The night before, in one of the most important games of the regular season, the Spurs were thumped 106–94 by their archrival, the Oklahoma City Thunder. The problem, however, was not the loss but the manner in which it had occurred. The game had started out promisingly, with the Spurs racing to a 20–9 lead. Then the team had imploded in a blizzard of misses and turn-overs, including several by guard Marco Belinelli. It added up to be precisely the kind of demoralizing loss the team wanted to avoid as the play-offs approached. Now, as practice begins, there is a tightness in the air, a taste of unease.

Gregg Popovich walks in. He's wearing a misshapen T-shirt from Jordan's Snack Bar in Ellsworth, Maine, and shorts a couple sizes too big. His hair is spare and frizzy, and he is carrying a paper plate with fruit and a plastic fork, his face set in a lopsided grin. He looks less like a commanding general than a disheveled uncle at a picnic. Then he sets down his plate and begins to move around the gym, talking to players. He touches them on the elbow, the shoulder, the arm. He chats in several languages. (The Spurs include players from seven countries.) He laughs. His eyes are bright, knowing, active. When he reaches Belinelli, his smile gets bigger and more lopsided. He exchanges a few words, and when Belinelli jokes back, they engage in a brief mock-wrestling match. It is a strange sight. A white-haired sixty-five-year-old coach wrestling a curly-haired six-foot-five Italian.

"I'm sure that was thought about beforehand," says R. C. Buford, the Spurs' general manager, who has worked with Popovich for twenty years. "He wanted to make sure Belinelli was okay. That's the way Pop approaches every relationship. He fills their cups."

When Popovich wants to connect with a player, he moves in tight enough that their noses nearly touch; it's almost like a challenge—an intimacy contest. As warm-ups continue, he keeps roving, connecting. A former player walks up, and Popovich beams, his face lighting up in a toothy grin. They talk for five minutes, catching up on life, kids, and teammates. "Love you, brother," Popovich says as they part.

"A lot of coaches can yell or be nice, but what Pop does is different," says assistant coach Chip Engelland. "He delivers two things over and over: He'll tell you the truth, with no bullshit, and then he'll love you to death."

Popovich's relationship with longtime Spurs star Tim Duncan is a case in point. Before selecting Duncan with the first overall pick in the 1997 draft, Popovich flew to Duncan's home in St. Croix, U.S. Virgin Islands, to meet the college star. They didn't just meet—they spent four days together traveling the island, visiting Duncan's family and friends, swimming in the ocean, and talking about everything under the sun except basketball. This is not a normal thing for coaches and players to do; most coaches and players interact in short, highly calculated bursts. But Popovich wanted to connect, to dig in and see if Duncan was the kind of person who was tough, unselfish, and humble enough to build a team around. Duncan and Popovich evolved into what amounts to a father-son relationship, a high-trust, no-bullshit connection that provides a vivid model for other players, especially when it comes to absorbing Popovich's high-volume truth-telling. As more than one Spur put it, If Tim can take Pop's coaching, how can I not take it?

A few minutes earlier the Spurs had gathered in the video room to review the Oklahoma City game. They had sat down with trepidation, expecting Popovich to detail the sins of the previous night, to show them what they did wrong and what they could do better. But when Popovich clicked on the video, the screen flickered with a CNN documentary on the fiftieth anniversary of the Voting Rights Act. The team watched in silence as the story unfolded: Martin Luther King, Jr., Lyndon Johnson, and the Selma marches. When it was over, Popovich asked questions. He always asks questions, and those questions are always the same: personal, direct, focused on the big picture. *What did you think of it? What would you have done in that situation?*

The players thought, answered, nodded. The room shifted and became something of a seminar, a conversation. They talked. They were not surprised because on the Spurs this kind of thing happens all the time. Popovich would create similar conversations on the war in Syria, or a change of government in Argentina, gay marriage, institutional racism, terrorism—it doesn't really matter, as long as it delivers the message he wants it to deliver: There are bigger things than basketball to which we are all connected.

"It's so easy to be insulated when you're a professional athlete," Buford says. "Pop uses these moments to connect us. He loves that we come from so many different places. That could pull us apart, but he makes sure that everybody feels connected and engaged to something bigger."

"Hug 'em and hold 'em" is the way Popovich often puts

it to his assistant coaches. "We gotta hug 'em and hold 'em."*

Much of that connection happens around the dinner table, as Popovich is obsessed with food and wine. His obsession can be gauged in a number of ways: the size of his home wine cellar, his part ownership of an Oregon vineyard, and the constant presence of the Food Network on his office television. But most of all it can be seen in the way he uses food and wine as a bridge to build relationships with players.

"Food and wine aren't just food and wine," Buford says. "They're his vehicle to make and sustain a connection, and Pop is really intentional about making that connection happen."

The Spurs eat together approximately as often as they play basketball together. First there are the team dinners, regular gatherings of all the players. Then there are smaller group dinners, handfuls of players getting together. Then there are the coach's dinners, which happen every night on the road before a game. Popovich plans them, picking the restaurants, sometimes two a night, to explore. (Staff joke: Bulimia is a job requirement.) These are not meals to be eaten and forgotten. At the end of the season, each coach gets a leather-bound keepsake book containing the menus and wine labels from every dinner.

---

* Popovich makes these connections in spite of the fact that—or perhaps because—he is a studious avoider of technology. He does not use his computer; his assistant prints out emails. While his staff persuaded him to buy an iPhone last year so that he could receive texts, he has yet to send one. He does all his communicating in person, up close.

"You'll be sitting on the plane, and all of a sudden a magazine lands on your lap, and you look up and it's Pop," says Sean Marks, a former Spurs assistant coach who's now general manager of the Brooklyn Nets. "He's circled some article about your hometown and wants to know if it's accurate, and where you like to eat, and what kind of wine you like to drink. And pretty soon he's suggesting places where you ought to eat, and he's making reservations for you and your wife or girlfriend. Then you go, and he wants to know all about it, what wine you had, what you ordered, and then there's another place to go. That's how it starts. And it never ends."

One misconception about highly successful cultures is that they are happy, lighthearted places. This is mostly not the case. They are energized and engaged, but at their core their members are oriented less around achieving happiness than around solving hard problems together. This task involves many moments of high-candor feedback, uncomfortable truth-telling, when they confront the gap between where the group is, and where it ought to be. Larry Page created one of these moments when he posted his "These ads suck" note in the Google kitchen. Popovich delivers such feedback to his players every day, usually at high volume. But how do Popovich and other leaders manage to give tough, truthful feedback without causing side effects of dissent and disappointment? What is the best feedback made of?

A few years back a team of psychologists from Stanford, Yale, and Columbia had middle school students write an essay, after which teachers provided different kinds of feedback. Researchers discovered that one particular form of feedback boosted student effort and performance so immensely that they deemed it "magical feedback." Students who received it chose to revise their papers far more often than students who did not, and their performance improved significantly. The feedback was not complicated. In fact, it consisted of one simple phrase.

I'm giving you these comments because I have very high expectations and I know that you can reach them.

That's it. Just nineteen words. None of these words contain any information on how to improve. Yet they are powerful because they deliver a burst of belonging cues. Actually, when you look more closely at the sentence, it contains three separate cues:

1. You are part of this group.
2. This group is special; we have high standards here.
3. I believe you can reach those standards.

These signals provide a clear message that lights up the unconscious brain: *Here is a safe place to give effort.* They also give us insight into the reason Popovich's methods are effective. His communications consist of three types of belonging cues.

- Personal, up-close connection (body language, attention, and behavior that translates as *I care about you*)

- Performance feedback (relentless coaching and criticism that translates as *We have high standards here*)
- Big-picture perspective (larger conversations about politics, history, and food that translate as *Life is bigger than basketball*)

Popovich toggles among the three signals to connect his team the way a skilled director uses a camera. First he zooms in close, creating an individualized connection. Then he operates in the middle distance, showing players the truth about their performance. Then he pans out to show the larger context in which their interaction is taking place. Alone, each of these signals would have a limited effect. But together they create a steady stream of magical feedback. Every dinner, every elbow touch, every impromptu seminar on politics and history adds up to build a relational narrative: *You are part of this group. This group is special. I believe you can reach those standards*. In other words, Popovich's yelling works, in part, because it is not just yelling. It is delivered along with a suite of other cues that affirm and strengthen the fabric of the relationships.

When you ask the Spurs about their greatest moment of team cohesion, many of them give the same strange answer. They mention a night not when the Spurs won but when they suffered their most painful loss.

It happened on June 18, 2013, in Miami. The Spurs were on the verge of winning their fifth NBA championship in a historic upset, having built a three-games-to-two lead in the best-of-seven series against the heavily favored Miami Heat. Going into the game, the Spurs were confident enough to plan for a possible celebration by booking a large private room at Il Gabbiano, one of their favorite restaurants.

From tip-off, game six was tight, and the lead swung back and forth. Then, toward the end of the fourth quarter, the Spurs went on a dramatic 8–0 run to take a 94–89 lead with 28.2 seconds left on the clock. The Heat sagged; the crowd went quiet. The championship seemed clinched. According to win-probability statistics, the odds of a Spurs victory at that point were 66:1. Along the edge of the court, security personnel started assembling, ropes in hand, to cordon off the court for the celebration. In the Spurs' locker room, attendants placed chilled champagne in ice tubs and taped up plastic sheeting over the lockers.

Then disaster.

LeBron James attempted a long shot and missed, but the Heat corralled the rebound and James made a three-pointer: 94–92. The Spurs were fouled and made one of two ensuing free throws, giving them a three-point lead with nineteen seconds left. Miami had one possession left to attempt to tie the game. The Spurs' defense dug in, pressuring the Heat and forcing James to try a long three-pointer, which missed badly. For a second, as the ball caromed high off the rim, the game seemed over. Then Miami's Chris Bosh snagged the rebound and flicked the ball to teammate Ray Allen in the corner. Allen stepped back and swished a three-pointer that seemed less like a basket than a dagger. Tie game. The contest went to overtime, where the newly energized Heat kept up the pressure. The final score was 103–100. The Spurs had gone from almost-certain victory to one of the most devastating defeats in NBA history.

The Spurs were in shock. Tony Parker sat with a towel over his head, crying. "I've never seen our team so broken," he said later. Tim Duncan lay on the floor, unable to move. Manu Ginobili could not look anyone in the face. "It was like death," said Sean Marks. "We were gutted."

Players and coaches naturally assumed the team would scrap the gathering at Il Gabbiano and go back to their hotel to regroup. But Popovich had other plans. "Pop's response was, 'Family!'" Brett Brown, then an assistant coach, later told a reporter. "'Everybody to the restaurant, straight there.'"

Popovich left before the team, taking a car with Marks. When they reached the empty restaurant, Popovich started working, preparing the space. He had the tables moved—he wanted the team together in the center, with coaches close by, surrounded by an outer ring of family. He started ordering appetizers, picking dishes that he knew his players would like. He chose wine and had the waiters open it. Then he sat down.

"He looked as sad as I've ever seen a person look," Marks recalls. "He's sitting in his chair, not saying a word, still devastated. Then—I know this sounds weird—but you can just see him make the shift and get past it. He takes a sip of wine and a deep breath. You can see him get over his emotions and start focusing on what the team needs. Right then the bus pulls up."

Popovich stood and greeted every player as they came through the door. Some got a hug, some got a smile, some got a joke or a light touch on the arm. The wine flowed. They sat and ate together. Popovich moved around the room, connecting with each player in turn. People later said he behaved like the father of a bride at a wedding, taking time with everyone, thanking them, appreciating them. There were no speeches, just a series of intimate conversations. In a moment that could have been filled with frustration, recrimination, and anger, he filled their cups. They talked about the game. Some of them cried. They began to come out of their private silences, to get past the loss and to connect. They even laughed.

"I remember watching him do that, and I couldn't believe it," R. C. Buford says. "By the end of the night, things felt almost normal. We were a team again. It's the single greatest thing I've ever seen in sports, bar none."*

---

* The Spurs went on to play game seven with cohesion and energy that surpassed their game six performance, though they ended up falling to Miami. The Spurs kept the unopened champagne and used it the following year after they defeated the Heat in five games to win their fifth championship.

5 How to Design for Belonging

The Architect of the Greenhouse

Tony Hsieh was no ordinary child. He was bright, playing four musical instruments and scoring straight As while barely cracking open a book. Hsieh (pronounced Shay) was also shy, preferring to spend his time in solitary thought rather than socializing. He liked puzzles; he loved the feeling of discovering creative solutions to difficult problems. His favorite TV show was *MacGyver,* whose hero was a resourceful secret agent who used everyday materials to escape impossible dilemmas and bring the bad guys to justice. This idea—that tough problems could be elegantly hacked—held enormous appeal. At an early age, he began to MacGyver his way through the world.

For example, when his parents told Hsieh to practice his piano, violin, trumpet, or French horn, he MacGyvered a method where he would record cassette tapes of his practice sessions, then play the recordings from behind the closed door of his bedroom so his unsuspecting parents thought he was dutifully at work. In high school, he MacGyvered the school's phone system into calling dial-a-porn for free (briefly elevating his popularity among the boys).

The pattern continued at Harvard, where Hsieh Mac-Gyvered studying (he assembled class notes and sold them for twenty dollars a pop) as well as late-night snacking (he bought pizza ovens and sold pizzas for less than the local outlet charged). After graduation, he cofounded a software company called Link Exchange, which he and his partners sold to Microsoft in 1998. At this point, he was twenty-five years old, he had millions of dollars in his pocket, and he would never have to work another day in his life. He began to look for something else to solve.

He found it in an online retailer called ShoeSite.com. On the surface, it did not seem like a particularly smart investment—after all, these were the unpromising early days of e-commerce, the bubble-burst era of failures like Pets .com. But Hsieh saw these failures as an opportunity to rewire a system. He thought about attempting a venture that would reinvent online retailing through a strong and distinctive company culture. He wanted to build an atmosphere of "fun and weirdness." The site would deliver not just shoes but what Hsieh called "personal emotional connections," both inside the company and out. A few months after making an initial investment, Hsieh became CEO. He renamed the company Zappos.

Things did not go well for Zappos at first. The business had trouble in the ways young businesses usually have trouble—supply, logistics, execution. At one point several staffers were living in Hsieh's San Francisco apartment. But in the early 2000s, things started to improve slowly, then with astonishing speed. In 2002, revenues were $32 million; in 2003, $70 million; in 2004, $184 million. The company relocated to Las Vegas and kept growing, reaching $1.1 billion in revenues in 2009. Zappos, which was sold to Amazon, now has fifteen hundred employees and $2 billion in revenue. It is consistently ranked among the country's top employee-friendly companies and attracts hundreds of applications for each available opening. It is easier to get into Harvard than to get a job at Zappos.

In 2009, Hsieh ventured beyond commerce to purchase the twenty-eight-acre block of downtown Las Vegas that surrounds Zappos headquarters, with the audacious idea of helping to revive it. This was not the glossy Las Vegas of the Strip; this was a desolate jumble of third-class casinos, empty parking lots, and run-down hotels that, as one observer put it, aspired to the category of blight. Here he set out to see if it was possible to MacGyver a city—that is, to use Zappos principles to rebuild a broken downtown.

Before meeting Hsieh, I visit his apartment, located on the twenty-third floor of a nearby building. I'm not alone; I'm accompanied by a dozen people and a guide. Hsieh, epitomizing the Zappos ethos of radical openness, allows groups of visitors to walk through his kitchen, his living room, his lush "jungle room" with walls and ceilings covered in plants, and the well-stocked bars, creating the strange intimacy of seeing a billionaire's half-eaten granola bar on the kitchen counter, his socks on the floor.

Then on his living room wall, we see the plan: a large satellite map of the Downtown Project, the borders marked in bright yellow, each lot designated with what looked to be an ever-changing set of possibilities. On an adjacent wall flutter several hundred colorful sticky notes scrawled with ideas for those lots: CREATIVE COMMONS ... EVERYTHING RUNS ON SOLAR ... DOG PARK ... TOWN HALL DISTILL-ERY ... COMMUNITY GARDEN. You get the feeling of an impossibly complex game being played—a Sim City unfolding in real time, with Hsieh as both designer and player.

An hour later, at a place called Container Park, we meet. He is a quiet man with a close-shaved head and a steady, attentive gaze. He picks his words with care, and if there's a pause in the conversation, he will wait with endless patience for you to fill it. Several people close to Hsieh describe him with the same metaphor: He's like an alien of superior intelligence who came to Earth and figured out what makes human beings tick. I ask him how this all happened.

"I try to help things happen organically," he says. "If you set things up right, the connection happens." He sits back and gestures at Container Park, the Downtown Project's newest crown jewel. A few months ago the place was an empty lot. Now it is a warm, welcoming gathering place built of colorful shipping containers that have been converted into shops and boutiques. Outside stands a giant metal sculpture of a praying mantis that emits fire through its antennae. Around us stroll hundreds of happy people enjoying the late-afternoon sunshine. Later tonight Sheryl Crow will play a concert in the park. While the Downtown Project has had its difficulties, its early phases have had some success: It's brought in $754 million in public and private projects, assisted ninety-two businesses, and infused the area with a new buzz.

We talk awhile, me asking questions, and Hsieh offering responses. It doesn't go particularly smoothly, in part because he seems to regard conversation as a hopelessly rudimentary tool for communication. A typical exchange goes something like this:

ME: How did you begin this project?
HSIEH: I like systems, I guess. [ten-second pause]
ME: What models and ideas inspired you?
HSIEH: A lot of different ideas, from different places. [twenty-second pause] That's a really hard question to answer.

He wasn't trying to be difficult; it was simply that words could not do the job. Then he suggested we go for a walk, and in an instant everything changed. He seemed to come alive as he moved around the streets, meeting people, talking to them, introducing them to me and to others. He had a connection with everyone, and more impressively, he sought to build connections between others. In the space of forty-five minutes, I saw him connect a movie director, a music-festival producer, an artist, the owner of a barbecue place, and three Zappos workers with someone they should talk to, a company they should check out, someone who shared their hobby, or an event they might be interested in. He was like a human version of a social app, and he made each connection with the same light, low-key, positive vibe. He had a gift of making these conversations seem utterly normal and, through that normalcy, special.

"He's very smart, but the smartest thing about him is that

he thinks sort of like an eight-year-old," says Jeanne Markel, director of culture for the Downtown Project. "He keeps things really simple and positive when it comes to people."

"I remember one time I was with him, and for some reason I got it in my head that we should have a Zappos blimp," says Joe Mahon, marketing manager of the Downtown Project. "Not some little blimp but a huge blimp, like the Goodyear blimp. It was a completely crazy idea, in retrospect. But Tony didn't bat an eye. I mean, he didn't hesitate for a second. He said, 'Good idea,' and we talked about it."

Beneath Hsieh's unconventional approach lies a mathematical structure based on what he calls collisions. Collisions—defined as serendipitous personal encounters—are, he believes, the lifeblood of any organization, the key driver of creativity, community, and cohesion. He has set a goal of having one thousand "collisionable hours" per year for himself and a hundred thousand collisionable hours per acre for the Downtown Project. This metric is why he closed a side entrance to Zappos headquarters, funneling people through a single entrance. And it's why, during a recent party, he started to get an uneasy feeling—people were standing around in isolated clusters, not mixing. He noticed that the furniture was blocking the flow, and a few seconds later he was heaving a large couch across the floor. Then he started moving lamps and tables, and before long he had completely rearranged the room. "It was the only time I've ever seen a billionaire move furniture," a friend jokes.

"This place is like a greenhouse," Hsieh says. "In some greenhouses, the leader plays the role of the plant that every other plant aspires to. But that's not me. I'm not the plant that everyone aspires to be. My job is to architect the greenhouse."

My job is to architect the greenhouse. This is a useful insight into how Hsieh creates belonging because it implies a process. "I probably say the word *collision* a thousand times a day," Hsieh says. "I'm doing this because the point isn't just about counting them but about making a mindset shift that they're what matters. When an idea becomes part of a language, it becomes part of the default way of thinking."

When you talk to people inside Hsieh's greenhouse, they seem as if they are under the influence of a powerful magnet. "It's not logical," says Dr. Zubin Damania, a radiologist who left a teaching position at Stanford to head up Hsieh's health clinic. "He's like Morpheus in the *Matrix* movie, where he gives you the pill where you really see the world for the first time."

"It's kind of impossible to explain," says Lisa Shufro, a Downtown Project staffer. "You connect with all these people, and you don't feel it in your head, you feel it in your stomach. It's a feeling of possibility, and he creates it wherever he goes."

"He knows how people connect so well that it's unconscious with him," says Maggie Hsu, who works on the Downtown Project's executive team. "At this point, he's been doing it so much that he almost can't help it. I've asked Tony over and over—why do people follow you around? Why do they respond to you? He says, 'I have no idea.'"

Hsu's story is typical. A few years ago she was a successful consultant at McKinsey when she heard about the Downtown Project. Curious, she sent an email, and Hsieh responded by inviting her out for a few days. Hsu showed up expecting the usual agenda of meetings, visits, and organized tours. What she got instead was a two-line email followed by a list of eight names.

Meet these people, Hsieh's note read. *Then ask them who else you should meet.*

Hsu was buffaloed. "I asked him, 'Is that it? Is there anything else I should do?' He said, 'You'll figure it out.' And he was right—it all sort of happened. It was like I was getting this signal that got stronger with everyone I talked to, and it was crazy strong, and I couldn't resist. I ended up moving here. It wasn't logical at all. It was like I had to do it."

We don't normally think about belonging to big groups in this way. Normally, when we think about belonging to big groups, we think about great communicators who create a vivid and compelling vision for others to follow. But that is not what's happening here. In fact, Hsieh is anticharismatic, he does not communicate particularly well, and his tools are grade school simple—*Meet people, you'll figure it out.* So why does it work so well?

During the Cold War, the United States and the Soviet Union conducted a decades-long, anything-goes race to build ever-more-powerful weapons and satellite systems. In both nations, inside hundreds of governmental and private enterprise projects, teams of engineers spent thousands of hours fervently working on complicated problems that nobody had ever attempted to solve before. Partway through that race, the U.S. government decided to look into the efficiency of this process. It solicited research into the question of why certain engineering projects were successful and others were not. One of the first people to formally attempt that research was a young MIT professor named Thomas Allen.

Allen wasn't a typical ivory tower academic; he was a middle-class kid from New Jersey who'd graduated from tiny Upsala College, then enlisted in the Marines during the Korean War. When he got out, he worked for Boeing, then went to MIT for dual graduate degrees in computer science and management, which left him perfectly positioned to pursue the government's request for research. ("I didn't even know they had a management degree when I got [to MIT]," he says. "I took a few classes, liked it, and some people talked me into getting a PhD.") Allen started his research by locating what he called "twin projects," where two or more engineering firms tackled the same complex challenge, such as figuring out how to guide an intercontinental ballistic missile or communicate with a satellite. He measured the quality of their solutions, then attempted to find the factors that successful projects had in common.

One pattern was immediately apparent: The most successful projects were those driven by sets of individuals who formed what Allen called "clusters of high communicators." The chemistry and cohesion within these clusters resembled that between Larry Page and Jeff Dean at Google. They had a knack for navigating complex problems with dazzling speed. Allen dug into the data to find out where the people in these clusters got their knack. Had they written for the same journals? Did they possess the same levels of intelligence? Were they the same age? Had they attended the same undergraduate schools or achieved the same level of degrees? Did they possess the most experience or the best leadership skills? All these factors would seem to make sense, but Allen could find none that played a meaningful role in cohesion. Except for one.

The distance between their desks.

At first he didn't believe it. Group chemistry is such a complex and mysterious process that he wanted the reason for it to be similarly complex and mysterious. But the more he explored the data, the clearer the answer became. What mattered most in creating a successful team had less to do with intelligence and experience and more to do with where the desks happened to be located.

"Something as simple as visual contact is very, very important, more important than you might think," Allen says. "If you can see the other person or even the area where they work, you're reminded of them, and that brings a whole bunch of effects."

Allen decided to dig deeper, measuring frequency of interactions against distance. "We could look at how often people communicated and see where they were located in relation to each other," he says. "We could see, just through the frequency, without knowing where they sat, who was on each floor. We were really surprised at how rapidly it decayed" when they moved to a different floor. "It turns out that vertical separation is a very serious thing. If you're on a different floor in some organizations, you may as well be in a different country."

When Allen plotted the frequency of interaction against distance, he ended up with a line that resembled a steep hill.

It was nearly vertical at the top and flat at the bottom. It became known as the Allen Curve.*

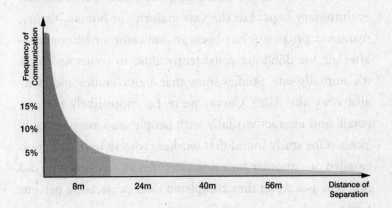

The key characteristic of the Allen Curve is the sudden steepness that happens at the eight-meter mark. At distances of less than eight meters, communication frequency rises off the charts. If our brains operated logically, we might expect the frequency and distance to change at a constant rate, producing a straight line. But as Allen shows, our brains do not operate logically. Certain proximities trigger huge changes in frequency of communication. Increase the distance to 50 meters, and communication ceases, as if a tap has been shut off. Decrease distance to 6 meters, and communication frequency skyrockets. In other words, proximity functions

* The Allen Curve echoes another famous social metric, the Dunbar Number, which reflects the cognitive limit to the number of people with whom we can have a stable social relationship (around 150). They would seem to underline the same truth: Our social brains are built to focus and respond to a relatively small number of people located within a finite distance of us. One hundred and fifty feet also happens to be the rough distance at which we can no longer recognize a face with the naked eye.

as a kind of connective drug. Get close, and our tendency to connect lights up.

As scientists have pointed out, the Allen Curve follows evolutionary logic. For the vast majority of human history, sustained proximity has been an indicator of belonging—after all, we don't get consistently close to someone unless it's mutually safe. Studies show that digital communications also obey the Allen Curve; we're far more likely to text, email, and interact virtually with people who are physically close. (One study found that workers who shared a location emailed one another four times as often as workers who did not, and as a result they completed their projects 32 percent faster.)

All of which gives us a lens to understand what Tony Hsieh is up to. He is leveraging the Allen Curve. His projects tend to succeed for the same reason the creative cluster projects succeeded: Closeness helps create efficiencies of connection. The people in his orbit behave as if they were under the influence of some kind of drug because, in fact, they are.

During our conversations, I ask Hsieh how he goes about recruiting new people into the Downtown Project. "If someone is interested, and we're interested in them, we invite them out here," he says. "We sort of do it in a sneaky way. We give them a place to stay for free and don't tell them too much. They get here and they hang out and see what's happening, and some of them decide to join. Things just sort of happen."

What percentage end up moving here?

He pauses for a long time. "Probably about one in twenty." At first, this number doesn't seem all that impressive—only

5 percent. Then you think about what's beneath that number. One hundred strangers will visit Hsieh, and after a few conversations and a handful of interactions, five will uproot themselves from their home and join this group they have just met. Hsieh has built a machine that transforms strangers into a tribe.

"It's funny how it happens," Hsieh says. "I never say very much; I don't make any big pitch. I just let them experience this place and wait for the moment to be right. Then I look at them and ask, 'So when are you moving to Vegas?'" He smiles. "And then some of them do."*

---

* Shortly after my reporting was completed, Downtown Project leaders embarked on a controversial series of belt-tightening moves, which resulted in the layoff of thirty staffers and Hsieh's pulling back from his leadership role. It remains to be seen whether this experiment can succeed in the long run.

6 Ideas for Action

Building safety isn't the kind of skill you can learn in a robotic, paint-by-numbers sort of way. It's a fluid, improvisational skill—sort of like learning to pass a soccer ball to a teammate during a game. It requires you to recognize patterns, react quickly, and deliver the right signal at the right time. And like any skill, it comes with a learning curve.

This learning curve applies even to the scientists who study belonging. For example, Will Felps, who did the bad apple study (see Chapter 1), described how insights from his research affected the way he communicated in his personal life. "I used to like to try to make a lot of small clever remarks in conversation, trying to be funny, sometimes in a cutting way," he says. "Now I see how negatively those signals can impact the group. So I try to show that I'm listening. When they're talking, I'm looking at their face, nodding, saying 'What do you mean by that,' 'Could you tell me more about this,' or asking their opinions about what we should do, drawing people out."

Amy Edmondson (whom we also met in Chapter 1) has studied psychological safety in a wide variety of workplaces. "I used to not think about whether I was making people safe at all," she says. "Now I think about it all the time, especially at the beginning of any interaction, and then I constantly check, especially if there's any change or tension. I bend over backward to make sure people are safe."

Felps and Edmondson are speaking to the same truth: Creating safety is about dialing in to small, subtle moments and delivering targeted signals at key points. The goal of this chapter is to provide a few tips on doing that.

Overcommunicate Your Listening: When I visited the successful cultures, I kept seeing the same expression on the faces of listeners. It looked like this: head tilted slightly forward, eyes unblinking, and eyebrows arched up. Their bodies were still, and they leaned toward the speaker with intent. The only sound they made was a steady stream of affirmations— *yes, uh-huh, gotcha*—that encouraged the speaker to keep going, to give them more. "Posture and expression are incredibly important," said Ben Waber, a former PhD student of Alex Pentland's who founded Humanyze, a social analytics consulting firm. "It's the way we prove that we're in sync with someone."

Relatedly, it's important to avoid interruptions. The smoothness of turn taking, as we've seen, is a powerful indicator of cohesive group performance. Interruptions shatter the smooth interactions at the core of belonging. They are so discohesive, in fact, that Waber uses interruption metrics as sales training tools. "When you can show someone numbers that the top salespeople hardly ever interrupt people, and then rate them on that scale, you can deliver a powerful message," he says. Of course, not all interruptions are negative: Creative sessions, for example, often contain bursts of interruptions. The key is to draw a distinction between interruptions born of mutual excitement and those rooted in lack of awareness and connection.

Spotlight Your Fallibility Early On—Especially If You're a Leader: In any interaction, we have a natural tendency to try to hide our weaknesses and appear competent. If you want to create safety, this is exactly the wrong move. Instead, you should open up, show you make mistakes, and invite input with simple phrases like "This is just my two cents." "Of course, I could be wrong here." "What am I missing?" "What do you think?"

R. C. Buford, general manager of the San Antonio Spurs, is one of the most successful executives in the history of sports. But if you watch him operate, you might mistake him for an assistant. He's a quiet, affable hound-dog Kansan who asks questions, listens keenly, and radiates humility. Early in our conversations, he brought up the looming retirements of several star players and said, "I'm absolutely terrified of the future." He could have talked about the organization's vaunted player selection and development systems, or the progress of the young players, or the smart trades they'd made, or the power of the culture they'd built. But he didn't do that—he said he was terrified. This kind of signal is not just an admission of weakness; it's also an invitation to create a deeper connection, because it sparks a response in the listener: *How can I help?*

"To create safety, leaders need to actively invite input," Edmondson says. "It's really hard for people to raise their hand and say, 'I have something tentative to say.' And it's equally hard for people not to answer a genuine question from a leader who asks for their opinion or their help."

Embrace the Messenger: One of the most vital moments for creating safety is when a group shares bad news or gives tough feedback. In these moments, it's important not simply to tolerate the difficult news but to embrace it. "You know the phrase 'Don't shoot the messenger'?" Edmondson says. "In fact, it's not enough to not shoot them. You have to hug the messenger and let them know how much you need that feedback. That way you can be sure that they feel safe enough to tell you the truth next time."*

Preview Future Connection: One habit I saw in successful groups was that of sneak-previewing future relationships,

---

* One way to detect belonging levels is by examining the kinds of personal language used in emails. A study by Lynn Wu of Wharton looked at two years of communication by eight thousand workers and showed that talking about sports, lunch, and coffee predicted whether an employee would be retained better than the revenue they brought in. A study by Amir Goldberg at Stanford showed that it was possible to predict how long employees stayed by how frequently their emails contained family references and swear words.

making small but telling connections between now and a vision of the future. The St. Louis Cardinals baseball team, for example, is renowned for their culture and their ability to develop young players into big-league talent. The Johnson City (Tennessee) Cardinals are St. Louis's lowest-level minor-league club. One day on a bus belonging to the Tennessee team, one of the Cardinals coaches, sitting in the front row, gestured up toward the television on which the big-league team was playing.

"You know that pitcher?"

Players looked up. On the screen, wearing a perfect white uniform, stood the heroic figure of Trevor Rosenthal, a young star who had become a dominant relief pitcher for the Cardinals; he had pitched in the previous year's World Series.

"Three years ago," the coach said, "he was sitting right in that seat where you are."

That's all he said. It wasn't much—it took about five seconds to deliver. But it was powerful, because it connected the dots between where the players were and where they were headed. *Three years ago he was sitting right in that seat where you are.*

Overdo Thank-Yous: When you enter highly successful cultures, the number of thank-yous you hear seems slightly over the top. At the end of each basketball season, for example, Spurs coach Gregg Popovich takes each of his star players aside and thanks them for allowing him to coach them. Those are his exact words: *Thank you for allowing me to coach you.* It makes little logical sense—after all, both

Popovich and the player are amply compensated, and it's not like the player had a choice whether to be coached. But this kind of moment happens all the time in highly successful groups, because it has less to do with thanks than affirming the relationship.

For example, when I visited KIPP Infinity, a remarkable charter school in Harlem, New York, I witnessed teachers thanking one another over and over. The math teachers received T-shirts marking Pi Day as a surprise present from the administrative assistant. Then Jeff Li, who teaches eighth-grade math, sent the following email to the other math teachers in the department:

> Dear math teachers I love,
> On Assessment #7, a mid-unit test on linear functions
> (part of the foundational major work of the grade),
> the class of 2024 has outperformed the previous two
> classes on essentially the same test. See below for the
> data.
>   Class of [2022]: 84.5
>   Class of 2023: 87.2
>   Class of 2024: 88.7
>   I know this is a result of better teaching at every
>   grade level from 5th grade on . . . so thanks for being
>   great teachers who are pushing to get better each year.
>   It's working!
>
> —Jeff

While all this thanking seems over the top, there's a strong scientific support that it ignites cooperative behavior. In a study by Adam Grant and Francesco Gino, subjects were asked to help a fictitious student named "Eric" write a cover letter for a job application. After helping him, half of the participants received a thankful response from Eric; half received a neutral response. The subjects then received a request for help from "Steve," a different student. Those who had received thanks from Eric chose to help Steve more than twice as often as those who had received the neutral response. In other words, a small thank-you caused people to behave far more generously to a completely different person. This is because thank-yous aren't only expressions of gratitude; they're crucial belonging cues that generate a contagious sense of safety, connection, and motivation.

In my research, I sometimes saw the most powerful person in a group publicly express gratitude for one of the group's least powerful members. For example, the chef Thomas Keller, who runs French Laundry, Per Se, and other world-class restaurants, has a habit of thanking the dishwasher at his restaurant openings, highlighting the fact that the performance of the restaurant depends on the person who performs the humblest task. Urban Meyer, who coached Ohio State football to a national championship in 2015, used this same method at the team's post-title celebration at Ohio Stadium, which was attended by tens of thousands of students and fans. Everyone presumed he would begin the celebration by introducing the star players who had led the team to success. Instead, Meyer introduced an unheralded player named Nik Sarac, a reserve defensive back who, at the beginning of the season, had voluntarily given up his scholarship so that Meyer could give it to a player who could help the team more. Meyer spotlighted Sarac for the same reason Keller spotlighted the dishwashers—*Here is the unheralded person who makes our success possible.*

Be Painstaking in the Hiring Process: Deciding who's in and who's out is the most powerful signal any group sends, and successful groups approach their hiring accordingly. Most have built lengthy, demanding processes that seek to assess fit, contribution (through deep background research and extensive interactions with a large number of people in the group), and performance (increasingly measured by tests). Some groups, like Zappos, have added an extra layer of belonging cues: after training is complete, they offer trainees a $2,000 bonus if they quit (about 10 percent of trainees accept the offer).

Eliminate Bad Apples: The groups I studied had extremely low tolerance for bad apple behavior and, perhaps more important, were skilled at naming those behaviors. The leaders of the New Zealand All-Blacks, the rugby squad that ranks as one of the most successful teams on the planet, achieve this through a rule that simply states "No Dickheads." It's simple, and that's why it's effective.

Create Safe, Collision-Rich Spaces: The groups I visited were uniformly obsessed with design as a lever for cohesion and interaction. I saw it in Pixar's Steve Jobs–designed atrium, and in the U.S. Navy's SEAL Team Six's expansive team rooms, which resemble hotel conference areas (albeit filled with extremely fit men with guns). I also saw it in smaller, simpler levers like coffee machines.

A few years back, Bank of America was struggling with burnout in its call center teams. They brought in Ben Waber to do a sociometric analysis, which found that workers were highly stressed and that the best reliever of that stress was time spent together away from their desks. Waber recommended aligning team members' schedules so they shared the same fifteen-minute coffee break every day. He also had the company buy nicer coffee machines and install them in more convenient gathering places. The effect was immediate: a 20 percent increase in productivity, and a reduction in turnover from 40 percent to 12 percent. Waber has also overseen interventions in company cafeterias: Merely replacing four-person tables with ten-person tables has boosted productivity by 10 percent. The lesson of all these studies is the same: Create spaces that maximize collisions.

"We used to hire out our food service to a contractor," said Ed Catmull, president and cofounder of Pixar (of whom we'll hear more in Chapter 16). "We didn't consider making food to be our core business. But when you hire it out, that food service company wants to make money, and the only way they can make money is to decrease the quality of the food or the service. They're not bad or greedy people; it's a structural problem. That's why we decided to take it over ourselves and give our people high-quality food at a reasonable price. Now we have really good food and people stay

here instead of leaving, and they have the kind of conversations and encounters that help our business. It's pretty
simple. We realized that food really is part of our core business."

Make Sure Everyone Has a Voice: Ensuring that everyone has a
voice is easy to talk about but hard to accomplish. This is
why many successful groups use simple mechanisms that encourage, spotlight, and value full-group contribution. For
example, many groups follow the rule that no meeting can
end without everyone sharing something.* Others hold regular reviews of recent work in which anybody can offer their
two cents. (Pixar calls them Dailies, all-inclusive morning
meetings where everybody gets the chance to offer input and
feedback on recently created footage.) Others establish regular forums where anyone can bring an issue or question
before the group's leaders, no matter how controversial it
might be. But no matter how strong the rule, the underlying
key is to have leaders who seek out connection and make
sure voices are heard.

A good example is the method of Michael Abrashoff, a
navy captain who took command of the destroyer *USS Benfold* in 1997. At the time, the *Benfold* ranked at the bottom

---

* My favorite method is Toyota's use of the *andon*, a cord that any employee can use to stop the assembly line when they spot a problem. Like
many organizational habits that ensure voice, this one seems inefficient at
first, overturning the hierarchy by allowing a lowly assembly-line worker to
stop the entire company. But a closer look shows that it creates belonging by
placing power and trust in the hands of the people doing the work.

of the navy's performance scores. One of his first acts was to hold one-on-ones with each of the ship's 310 sailors for thirty minutes. (Completing all the meetings took about six weeks.) Abrashoff asked each sailor three questions:

1. What do you like most about the *Benfold*?
2. What do you like least?
3. What would you change if you were captain?

Whenever Abrashoff received a suggestion he felt was immediately implementable, he announced the change over the ship's intercom, giving credit to the idea's originator. Over the next three years, on the strength of this and other measures (which are detailed in Abrashoff's book *It's Your Ship*), the *Benfold* rose to become one of the navy's highest-ranked ships.

Pick Up Trash: Back in the mid-1960s, UCLA's men's basketball team was in the midst of one of the most successful eras in sports history, winning ten titles in twelve years. Franklin Adler, the team's student manager, saw something odd: John Wooden, the team's legendary head coach, was picking up trash in the locker room. "Here was a man who had already won three national championships," Adler said, "a man who was already enshrined in the Hall of Fame as a player, a man who had created and was in the middle of a dynasty— bending down and picking up scraps from the locker room floor."

Wooden was not alone. Ray Kroc, the founder of McDonald's, was famous for picking up trash. "Every night you'd see him coming down the street, walking close to the gutter, picking up every McDonald's wrapper and cup along the way," former McDonald's CEO Fred Turner told author Alan Deutschman. "He'd come into the store with both hands full of cups and wrappers. I saw Ray spend one Saturday morning with a toothbrush cleaning out holes in the mop wringer. No one else really paid attention to the damned mop wringer, because everyone knew it was just a mop bucket. But Kroc saw all the crud building up in the holes, and he wanted to clean them so the wringer would work better."

I kept seeing that pattern. Coach Billy Donovan of the University of Florida (now with the Oklahoma City Thunder) cleaned up Gatorade that had spilled on the floor. Mike Krzyzewski of Duke and Tom Coughlin of the New York Giants did the same. The leaders of the All-Blacks rugby team have formalized this habit into a team value called "sweeping the sheds." Their leaders do the menial work, cleaning and tidying the locker rooms—and along the way vividly model the team's ethic of togetherness and teamwork.

This is what I would call a muscular humility—a mindset of seeking simple ways to serve the group. Picking up trash is one example, but the same kinds of behaviors exist around allocating parking places (egalitarian, with no special spots reserved for leaders), picking up checks at meals (the leaders do it every time), and providing for equity in salaries, particularly for start-ups. These actions are powerful not just because they are moral or generous but also because they send a larger signal: *We are all in this together.*

Capitalize on Threshold Moments: When we enter a new group, our brains decide quickly whether to connect. So successful cultures treat these threshold moments as more important than any other. For example, suppose you are hired at Pixar, whether it's as a director or as a barista in the company café. On your first day, you and a small group of fellow newbies are ushered into the theater where screenings are held. You are asked to sit in the fifth row—because that's where the directors sit. Then you hear the following words: *Whatever you were before, you are a filmmaker now. We need you to help us make our films better.* "It's incredibly powerful," said Mike Sundy, who works in data management. "You feel changed."

The Oklahoma City Thunder, a successful NBA team, makes similar use of their first day. Oklahoma City is an unlikely place for a professional sports franchise: It is relatively small and isolated, known more for tornadoes than for nightlife. When you are hired by the Thunder, either as a player or as an employee, the first thing that happens is that you are taken to the Oklahoma City National Memorial, which honors the victims of the 1995 Oklahoma City bombing. You walk around the reflecting pool. You see the sculpture of 168 chairs, one for each victim.

* Samantha Wilson, who was originally hired by Pixar as a barista for the company café, is now a story manager for the studio, having worked on *Inside Out, Up,* and *Cars 2.*

The general manager, Sam Presti, often leads the tour. He doesn't say much; he simply lets you walk around and feel the solemnity of the place. Then, toward the end, he reminds players to look into the stands during games and to remember that many of those people were personally affected by this tragedy. It's a small moment. But it makes a big difference for the same reason the WIPRO experiment made a difference. It sends a powerful belonging cue at the precise moment when people are ripest to receive it.

Of course, threshold moments don't only happen on day one; they happen every day. But the successful groups I visited paid attention to moments of arrival. They would pause, take time, and acknowledge the presence of the new person, marking the moment as special: *We are together now.*

Avoid Giving Sandwich Feedback: In many organizations, leaders tend to deliver feedback using the traditional sandwich method: You talk about a positive, then address an area that needs improvement, then finish with a positive. This makes sense in theory, but in practice it often leads to confusion, as people tend to focus either entirely on the positive or entirely on the negative.

In the cultures I visited, I didn't see many feedback sandwiches. Instead, I saw them separate the two into different processes. They handled negatives through dialogue, first by asking if a person wants feedback, then having a learning-focused two-way conversation about the needed growth. They handled positives through ultraclear bursts of recognition and praise. The leaders I spent time with shared a capacity for radiating delight when they spotted behavior worth praising. These moments of warm, authentic happiness functioned as magnetic north, creating clarity, boosting belonging, and orienting future action.

Embrace Fun: This obvious one is still worth mentioning, because laughter is not just laughter; it's the most fundamental sign of safety and connection.

Skill 2

Share Vulnerability

7

"Tell Me What You Want, and I'll Help You"

On July 10, 1989, United Airlines flight 232 left Denver and headed for Chicago with 285 passengers on board. The weather was sunny and mild, with light winds out of the west at thirteen miles per hour. For the first hour and ten minutes of the trip, everything went perfectly. Over Iowa, the crew, consisting of Captain Al Haynes, first officer Bill Records, and flight engineer Dudley Dvorak, put the plane on autopilot, ate lunch, and shot the breeze. Haynes, fifty-seven, was good at shooting the breeze. A low-key Texan and a former Marine, he had an amiable manner appreciated by his crews. Two years from retirement, he was planning for the next stage of life, when he would pilot an RV around the country with his wife, Darlene.

Then, at 3:16, came a loud explosion from the tail. The plane shook fiercely, then started climbing and tilting hard to the right. Records grabbed one of the two control wheels, known as yokes, and said, "I have the airplane." Checking the gauges, the crew realized the plane's tail engine—one of the DC-10's three engines—was gone. Meanwhile the plane kept tilting farther to the right despite Records's efforts to correct it.

"Al," Records said, trying to keep his voice calm, "I can't control the airplane."

Haynes seized his yoke. "I got it," he said, but he didn't have it. He pulled with all his strength, but the controls barely budged. The plane kept tilting to the right, until it felt like it was nearly standing on the wing.

Later investigators would trace the explosion to a microscopic crack in a six-foot-diameter fan inside the tail engine. The consequences of the explosion, however, went beyond the loss of the engine, which could normally be overcome. Shrapnel had sliced the main and backup hydraulic control lines through which the pilots operated the rudder, ailerons, and wing flaps—in short, the explosion removed the pilots' ability to control the plane.

The term the National Transportation Safety Board uses for this type of event is *catastrophic failure*. Airlines didn't bother training pilots for catastrophic failure for two reasons. First, such failures are extremely rare—the odds of losing hydraulics *and* backups had been calculated at one in a billion. Second, they are invariably fatal.

Haynes managed to stop the roll by using the throttles to increase power to the right-wing engine and decrease power to the left-wing engine. The asymmetric thrust helped the plane to slowly tilt back to a rough semblance of level flight. But it did nothing to fix the bigger problem: The controls wouldn't budge. The plane was now wobbling through the Iowa sky like a poorly made paper airplane, porpoising up and down thousands of feet each minute. Haynes and Records continued to wrestle with the yokes. The flight stewards moved through the cabin, trying to restore calm. One family took out a Bible and began to pray.

In an aisle seat of first class, a forty-six-year-old man named Denny Fitch was cleaning up the coffee that had spilled on his lap when the explosion happened. Fitch worked for United as a pilot trainer. He spent his days in a flight simulator, teaching pilots how to handle emergencies. Now he spoke with a flight attendant and asked her to inform the captain of his willingness to help. The word came back: *Send him up*. Fitch walked up the aisle, opened the cockpit door, and his heart dropped.

"The scene to me as a pilot was unbelievable," Fitch later told a reporter. "Both the pilots were in short-sleeved shirts, the tendons being raised on their forearms, their knuckles were white. . . . The first thing that strikes your mind is, 'Dear God, I'm going to die this afternoon.' The only question that remains is, 'How long is it going to take Iowa to hit me?'"

Fitch scanned the gauges, trying to make sense of them. He had never seen a complete hydraulic failure before, and like the pilots, he was having trouble comprehending what was going on. Flight engineer Dvorak was on the radio to United's maintenance seeking advice. It was a moment of peak confusion.

"Tell me," Fitch said to Haynes. "Tell me what you want, and I'll help you."

Haynes gestured to the engine throttles that were located on the console between the two pilots. As Haynes and Records had their hands full wrestling with the yokes, someone needed to run the throttles to try to maintain level flight. Fitch moved forward, knelt between the seats, and grasped the throttles with both hands.

Shoulder to shoulder, the three men began to do something that no pilots had ever done: fly a DC-10 without any controls. They began to communicate in a particular way, through short, urgent bursts.

HAYNES: Okay, let's start this sucker down a little more.

FITCH: Okay, set your power a little bit.

HAYNES: Anybody have any ideas about [what to do about the landing gear]? He [Dvorak] is talking to [maintenance].

FITCH: [Dvorak] is talking to [maintenance]. I'm gonna alternate-gear you. Maybe that will even help you. If there is no fluid, I don't know how outboard ailerons are going to help you.

HAYNES: How do you, we get gear down?

FITCH: Well, they can free-fall. The only thing is, we alternate the gear. We got the [landing gear] doors down?

HAYNES: Yep.

RECORDS: We're gonna have trouble stopping too.

HAYNES: Oh yeah. We don't have any brakes.

RECORDS: No brakes?

HAYNES: Well, we have some brakes [but not much].

FITCH: [Braking will be a] one-shot deal. Just mash it, mash it once. That's all you get. I'm gonna turn you.

[I'm gonna] give you a left turn back to the airport. Is that okay?

HAYNES: I got it.

[A few minutes later.]

HAYNES: A little left bank. Back, back.

FITCH: Hold this thing level if you can.

HAYNES: Level, baby, level, level . . .

DVORAK: We're turning now.

FITCH: More power, more power, give 'em more power.

RECORDS: More power, full power.

FITCH: Power picks 'em up.

UNKNOWN VOICE: Right turn, throttle back.

HAYNES: Can we turn left?

DVORAK (speaking to Fitch): Do you want this seat?

FITCH: Yes, do you mind?

DVORAK: I don't mind. I think that you know what you're doing there. . . .

The term pilots use to describe this type of short-burst communication is *notifications*. A notification is not an order or a command. It provides context, telling of something noticed, placing a spotlight on one discrete element of the world. Notifications are the humblest and most primitive form of communication, the equivalent of a child's finger-point: *I see this*. Unlike commands, they carry unspoken questions: *Do you agree? What else do you see?* In a typical landing or takeoff, a proficient crew averages twenty notifications per minute.

During their interactions after the explosion, the makeshift crew of Flight 232 communicated at a rate of more than sixty notifications per minute. Some of the interactions consisted of big, open-ended questions, mostly asked by Haynes. *How do we get the [landing] gear down? . . . Anybody have any ideas?* These are not the kinds of questions one would normally expect a captain to ask. In fact, they're the opposite. Normally, a captain's job in an emergency is to be in command and to project capability and coolness. Yet over and over Haynes notified his crew of a very different truth: *Your captain has no idea what is going on or how to fix it. Can you help?*

This combination of notifications and open-ended questions added up to a pattern of interaction that was neither smooth nor graceful. It was clunky, unconfident, and full of repetitions. Conceptually, it resembled a person feeling his way through a dark room, sensing obstacles and navigating fitfully around them. *We're gonna have trouble stopping too. . . . Oh yeah. We don't have any brakes. . . . No brakes? . . . Well, we have some brakes. . . . Just mash it, mash it once.*

Interacting in this stilted, unconfident fashion, the crew of Flight 232 solved a complex series of problems while flying at four hundred miles per hour. They figured out how to optimally distribute power between the two engines and how to try to anticipate the porpoising movements the plane was making. They communicated with the cabin, attendants, passengers, flight control, maintenance, and emergency crews on the ground. They chose routes, calculated descent rates, prepared for evacuation, and even cracked jokes. As they got closer to Sioux City, the air traffic controller cleared them to land on any of the airport's runways. Haynes chuckled and asked, "You want to be particular and make it a runway, huh?" Everyone laughed.

A few minutes later, flying at twice the normal landing speed and descending at six times the normal rate, Flight 232 attempted to land. A wingtip dipped and dug into the runway, sending the plane into a fiery cartwheel. The crash was terrible, but 185 people survived, including the entire crew. Some walked out of the wreckage into a cornfield. The survival of so many passengers was termed a miracle.

In the weeks afterward, as part of its investigation, the National Transportation Safety Board placed experienced crews in simulators and re-created the conditions faced by Flight 232 at the moment it lost all hydraulics. The simulation was run twenty-eight times. All twenty-eight times, the planes crashed, spiraling to the ground without getting close to Sioux City.

All of which underlines a strange truth. The crew of Flight 232 succeeded not because of their individual skills but because they were able to combine those skills into a greater intelligence. They demonstrated that a series of small, humble exchanges—*Anybody have any ideas? Tell me what you want, and I'll help you*—can unlock a group's ability to perform. The key, as we're about to learn, involves the willingness to perform a certain behavior that goes against our every instinct: sharing vulnerability.

So far we've spent this book in what you might call the glue department, exploring how successful groups create belonging. Now we'll turn our attention to the muscle, to see how successful groups translate connection into trusting cooperation.

When you watch highly cohesive groups in action, you will see many moments of fluid, trusting cooperation. These moments often happen when the group is confronted with a tough obstacle—for example, a SEAL team navigating a training course, or an improv comedy team navigating a sketch. Without communication or planning, the group starts to move and think as one, finding its way through the obstacle in the same way that a school of fish finds its way through a coral reef, as if they are all wired into the same brain. It's beautiful.

If you look closely, however, you will also notice something else. Sprinkled amid the smoothness and fluency are moments that don't feel so beautiful. These moments are clunky, awkward, and full of hard questions. They contain pulses of profound tension, as people deal with hard feedback and struggle together to figure out what is going on. What's more, these moments don't happen by accident. They happen by design.

At Pixar, those uncomfortable moments happen in what they call BrainTrust meetings. The BrainTrust is Pixar's method of assessing and improving its movies during their development. (Each film is BrainTrusted about half a dozen times, at regular intervals.) The meeting brings the film's director together with a handful of the studio's veteran directors and producers, all of whom watch the latest version of the movie and offer their candid opinion. From a distance, the BrainTrust appears to be a routine huddle. Up close, it's more like a painful medical procedure—specifically, a dissection that spotlights, names, and analyzes the film's flaws in breathtaking detail.

A BrainTrust meeting is not fun. It is where directors are told that their characters lack heart, their storylines are confusing, and their jokes fall flat. But it's also where those movies get better. "The BrainTrust is the most important thing we do by far," said Pixar president Ed Catmull. "It depends on completely candid feedback."

In rhythm and tone, BrainTrust meetings resemble the atmosphere inside the cockpit of Flight 232. They consist of a steady stream of here's-the-bad-news notifications accompanied by a few big, scary questions—*Does anybody know how to land this thing?* Participants spend most of the time in a state of brow-furrowing struggle as they grapple with the fact that the movie, at the moment, isn't working. "All our movies suck at first," Catmull says. "The BrainTrust is where we figure out why they suck, and it's also where they start to not suck."

At the Navy SEALs, such uncomfortable, candor-filled moments happen in the After-Action Review, or AAR. The AAR is a gathering that takes place immediately after each mission or training session: Team members put down their weapons, grab a snack and water, and start talking. As in BrainTrusts, the team members name and analyze problems and face uncomfortable questions head-on: *Where did we fail? What did each of us do, and why did we do it? What will we do differently next time?* AARs can be raw, painful, and filled with pulses of emotion and uncertainty.

"They're not real fun," said Christopher Baldwin, a former operator with SEAL Team Six. "They can get tense at times. I've never seen people fistfight, but it can get close. Still, it's probably the most crucial thing we do together, aside from the missions themselves, because that's where we figure out what really happened and how to get better."

While the SEALs and Pixar generate these moments in a structured way, other groups use looser, more organic methods. At Gramercy Tavern, a New York restaurant whose staff ranks as the culinary world's version of a SEAL team, I watched as Whitney Macdonald was minutes away from a moment she had long anticipated: her first-ever shift as a front waiter. The lunch crowd was lining up on the sidewalk, and she was excited and a bit nervous.

Assistant general manager Scott Reinhardt approached her—for a pep talk, I presumed.

I was wrong. "Okay," Reinhardt said, fixing Whitney with a bright, penetrating gaze. "The one thing we know about today is that it's not going to go perfectly. I mean, it *could,* but odds are really, really, really high that it won't."

A flicker of surprise traveled across Whitney's face. She had trained for six months for this day, learning every painstaking detail of the job, hoping to perform well. She had worked as a back server, taken notes, sat in on lineup meetings, and shadowed shift after shift. Now she was being told in no uncertain terms that she was destined to screw up.

"So here's how we'll know if you had a good day," Reinhardt continued. "If you ask for help ten times, then we'll know it was good. If you try to do it all alone . . ." His voice trailed off, the implication clear—*It will be a catastrophe.*

On the face of it, these awkward moments at Pixar, the

SEALs, and Gramercy Tavern don't make sense. These groups seem to intentionally create awkward, painful interactions that look like the opposite of smooth cooperation. The fascinating thing is, however, these awkward, painful interactions generate the highly cohesive, trusting behavior necessary for smooth cooperation. Let's look deeper into how this happens.

8

The Vulnerability Loop

Imagine that you and a stranger ask each other the following two sets of questions.

SET A

- What was the best gift you ever received and why?
- Describe the last pet you owned.
- Where did you go to high school? What was your high school like?
- Who is your favorite actor or actress?

SET B

- If a crystal ball could tell you the truth about yourself, your life, the future, or anything else, what would you want to know?
- Is there something that you've dreamed of doing for a long time? Why haven't you done it?
- What is the greatest accomplishment of your life?
- When did you last sing to yourself? To someone else?

At first glance, the two sets of questions have a lot in common. Both ask you to disclose personal information, to tell stories, to share. However, if you were to do this experiment (its full form contains thirty-six questions), you would notice two differences. The first is that as you went through Set B, you would feel a bit apprehensive. Your heart rate would increase. You would be more uncomfortable. You would blush, hesitate, and perhaps laugh out of nervousness. (It is not easy, after all, to tell a stranger something important you've dreamed of doing all your life.)

The second difference is that Set B would make you and the stranger feel closer to each other—around 24 percent closer than Set A, according to experimenters.* While Set A allows you to stay in your comfort zone, Set B generates confession, discomfort, and authenticity that break down barriers between people and tip them into a deeper connection. While Set A generates information, Set B generates something more powerful: vulnerability.

At some level, we intuitively know that vulnerability tends to spark cooperation and trust. But we may not realize how powerfully and reliably this process works, particularly when it comes to group interactions. So it's useful to meet Dr. Jeff Polzer, a professor of organizational behavior at Harvard who has spent a large chunk of his career examin-

---

* The questions were developed by psychologists Arthur and Elaine Aron. In its full form, the Experimental Generation of Interpersonal Closeness also includes four minutes of silent gazing into each other's eyes. The original experiment was done with seventy-one pairs of strangers, and one pair ended up marrying. (They invited the entire lab to the ceremony.)

ing how small, seemingly insignificant social exchanges can create cascade effects in groups.

"People tend to think of vulnerability in a touchy-feely way, but that's not what's happening," Polzer says. "It's about sending a really clear signal that you have weaknesses, that you could use help. And if that behavior becomes a model for others, then you can set the insecurities aside and get to work, start to trust each other and help each other. If you never have that vulnerable moment, on the other hand, then people will try to cover up their weaknesses, and every little microtask becomes a place where insecurities manifest themselves."

Polzer points out that vulnerability is less about the sender than the receiver. "The second person is the key," he says. "Do they pick it up and reveal their own weaknesses, or do they cover up and pretend they don't have any? It makes a huge difference in the outcome." Polzer has become skilled at spotting the moment when the signal travels through the group. "You can actually see the people relax and connect and start to trust. The group picks up the idea and says, 'Okay, this is the mode we're going to be in,' and it starts behaving along those lines, according to the norm that it's okay to admit weakness and help each other."

The interaction he describes can be called a vulnerability loop. A shared exchange of openness, it's the most basic building block of cooperation and trust. Vulnerability loops seem swift and spontaneous from a distance, but when you look closely, they all follow the same discrete steps:

1. Person A sends a signal of vulnerability.
2. Person B detects this signal.

3. Person B responds by signaling their own vulnerability.
4. Person A detects this signal.
5. A norm is established; closeness and trust increase.

Consider the situation of Al Haynes on Flight 232. He was the captain of the plane, the source of power and authority to whom everyone looked for reassurance and direction. When the explosion knocked out the controls, his first instinct was to play that role—to grab the yoke and say, "I got it." (Later he would call those three words "the dumbest thing I've ever said in my life.") Had he continued interacting with his crew in this way, Flight 232 would have likely crashed. But he did not continue on that path. He was able to do something even more difficult: to send a signal of vulnerability, to communicate to his crew that he needed them. It took just four words:

Anybody have any ideas?

Likewise, when pilot trainer Denny Fitch entered the cockpit, he could have attempted to issue commands and take charge—after all, he knew as much, if not more, about emergency procedures as Haynes did. Instead, he did the opposite: He explicitly put himself beneath Haynes and the crew, signaling his role as helper:

Tell me what you want, and I'll help you.

Each of these small signals took only a few seconds to deliver. But they were vital, because they shifted the dynamic, allowing two people who had been separate to function as one.

It's useful to zoom in on this shift. As it happens, scientists have designed an experiment to do exactly that, called the Give-Some Game. It works like this: You and another person, whom you've never met, each get four tokens. Each token is worth a dollar if you keep it but two dollars if you give it to the other person. The game consists of one decision: How many tokens do you give the other person?

This is not a simple decision. If you give all, you might end up with nothing. If you're like most people, you end up giving an average of 2.5 tokens to a stranger—slightly biased toward cooperation. What gets interesting, however, is how people tend to behave when their vulnerability levels are increased a few notches.

In one experiment, subjects were asked to deliver a short presentation to a roomful of people who had been instructed by experimenters to remain stone-faced and silent. They played the Give-Some Game afterward. You might imagine that the subjects who endured this difficult experience would respond by becoming less cooperative, but the opposite turned out to be true: the speakers' cooperation levels increased by 50 percent. That moment of vulnerability did not reduce willingness to cooperate but boosted it. The inverse was also true: Increasing people's sense of power—that is, tweaking a situation to make them feel more invulnerable—dramatically diminished their willingness to cooperate.

The link between vulnerability and cooperation applies not only to individuals but also to groups. In an experiment by David DeSteno of Northeastern University, participants were asked to perform a long, tedious task on a computer that was rigged to crash just as they were completing it. Then one of their fellow participants (who was actually a confederate of the researchers) would walk over, notice the problem, and generously spend time "fixing" the computer, thereby rescuing the participant from having to reload the data. Afterward the participants played the Give-Some Game. As you might expect, the subjects were significantly more cooperative with the person who fixed their computer. But here's the thing: They were equally cooperative with complete strangers. In other words, the feelings of trust and closeness sparked by the vulnerability loop were transferred in full strength to someone who simply happened to be in the room. The vulnerability loop, in other words, is contagious.

"We feel like trust is stable, but every single moment your brain is tracking your environment, and running a calculation whether you can trust the people around you and bond with them," says DeSteno. "Trust comes down to context. And what drives it is the sense that you're vulnerable, that you need others and can't do it on your own."

Normally, we think about trust and vulnerability the way we think about standing on solid ground and leaping into the unknown: first we build trust, *then* we leap. But science is showing us that we've got it backward. Vulnerability doesn't come after trust—it precedes it. Leaping into the unknown, when done alongside others, causes the solid ground of trust to materialize beneath our feet.

Question: How would you go about finding ten large red balloons deployed at secret locations throughout the United States?

This is not an easy question. It was dreamed up by scientists from the Defense Advanced Research Projects Agency (DARPA), a division of the U.S. Department of Defense tasked with helping America's military prepare for future technological challenges. The Red Balloon Challenge, which DARPA announced on October 29, 2009, was designed to mimic real-life dilemmas like terrorism and disease control, and offered a $40,000 prize to the first group to accurately locate all ten balloons. The immensity of the task—ten balloons in 3.1 million square miles—led some to wonder if DARPA had gone too far. A senior analyst for the National Geospatial-Intelligence Agency declared it "impossible."

Within days of the announcement, hundreds of groups signed up, representing a diverse cross-section of America's brightest minds: hackers, social media entrepreneurs, tech companies, and research universities. The vast majority took a logical approach to the problem: They built tools to attack it. They constructed search engines to analyze satellite photography technology, tapped into existing social and business networks, launched publicity campaigns, built open-source intelligence software, and nurtured communities of searchers on social media.

The team from MIT Media Lab, on the other hand, didn't do any of that stuff because they didn't find out about the challenge until four days before launch. A group of students, led by postdoctoral fellow Riley Crane, realized they had no time to assemble a team or create technology or do anything that resembled an organized approach. So instead they took a different tack. They built a website that consisted of the following invitation:

When you sign up to join the MIT Red Balloon Challenge Team, you'll be provided with a personalized invitation link, like http://balloon.mit.edu/yournamehere

Have all your friends sign up using your personalized invitation. If anyone you invite, or anyone they invite, or anyone they invite (. . . and so on) wins money, so will you!

We're giving $2000 per balloon to the first person to send us the correct coordinates, but that's not all—we're also giving $1000 to the person who invited them. Then we're giving $500 [to] whoever invited the inviter, and $250 to whoever invited them, and so on . . . (see how it works).

Compared to the sophisticated tools and technology deployed by other groups, the MIT team's approach was laughably primitive. They had no organizational structure or strategy or software, not even a map of the United States to help locate the balloons. This wasn't a well-equipped team; it was closer to a hastily scrawled plea shoved into a bottle and lobbed into the ocean of the Internet: "If you find this, please help!"

On the morning of December 3, two days before the balloon launch, MIT switched on the website. For a few hours, nothing happened. Then, at 3:42 P.M. on December 3, people began to join. Connections first bloomed out of Boston, then exploded, radiating to Chicago, Los Angeles, San Francisco, Minneapolis, Denver, Texas, and far beyond, including Europe. Viewed in time lapse, the spread of connections resembled the spontaneous assembly of a gigantic nervous system, with hundreds of new people joining the effort with each passing hour.

At precisely 10:00 A.M. Eastern on December 5, DARPA launched the balloons in secret locations ranging from Union Square in downtown San Francisco to a baseball field outside Houston, Texas, to a woodland park near Christiana, Delaware. Thousands of teams swung into action, and the organizers settled in for a long wait: They estimated it would take up to a week for a team to accurately locate all ten balloons.

Eight hours, fifty-two minutes, and forty-one seconds later, it was over. The MIT team had found all ten balloons and had done so with the help of 4,665 people—or as DARPA organizer Peter Lee put it, "a huge amount of participation from shockingly little money." Their primitive, last-minute, message-in-a-bottle method had defeated better-equipped attempts, creating a fast, deep wave of motivated teamwork and cooperation.

The reason was simple. All the other teams used a logical, incentive-based message: *Join us on this project, and you might win money.* This signal sounds motivating, but it doesn't really encourage cooperation—in fact, it does the opposite. If you tell others about the search, you are slightly reducing your chances of winning prize money. (After all, if others find the balloon and you don't, they'll receive the entire reward.) These teams were asking for participants' vulnerability, while remaining invulnerable themselves.

The MIT team, on the other hand, signaled its own vulnerability by promising that everyone connected to finding a red balloon would share in the reward. Then it provided people with the opportunity to create networks of vulnerability by reaching out to their friends, then asking them to reach out to *their* friends. The team did not dictate what participants should do or how they should do it, or give them specific tasks to complete or technology to use. It simply gave out the link and let people do with it what they pleased. And what they pleased, it turned out, was to connect with lots of other people. Each invitation created another vulnerability loop that drove cooperation—*Hey, I'm doing this crazy balloon-hunting project and I need your help.*

What made the difference in cooperation, in other words, wasn't how many people a person reached or how good their balloon-search technology was—it wasn't really about a given individual at all. It was rather about how effectively people created relationships of mutual risk. The Red Balloon Challenge wasn't even really a technology contest. It was, like all endeavors that seek to create cooperation, a vulnerability-sharing contest.

The story of the Red Balloon Challenge strikes us as surprising, because most of us instinctively see vulnerability as a condition to be hidden. But science shows that when it comes to creating cooperation, vulnerability is not a risk but a psychological requirement.

"What are groups really for?" Polzer asks. "The idea is that we can combine our strengths and use our skills in a complementary way. Being vulnerable gets the static out of the way and lets us do the job together, without worrying or hesitating. It lets us work as one unit."

After talking to Polzer and other scientists who study

trust, I began to see vulnerability loops in other places I visited. Sometimes they were small, quick exchanges. A pro baseball coach began a season-opening speech to his players by saying, "I was so nervous about talking to you today," and the players responded by smiling sympathetically—they were nervous too. Sometimes these loops took the form of physical objects, like the Failure Wall that Dun & Bradstreet Credibility Corporation built, a whiteboard where people could share moments where they'd fallen short.

Sometimes they were habits of seemingly invulnerable leaders, such as Apple founder Steve Jobs's penchant for beginning conversations with the phrase, "Here's a dopey idea." ("And sometimes they were," recalls Jonathan Ive, Apple's senior vice president of design, in his memorial to Jobs. "Really dopey. Sometimes they were truly dreadful.") Each loop was different, yet they shared a deeper pattern: an acknowledgment of limits, a keen awareness of the group nature of the endeavor. The signal being sent was the same: *You have a role here. I need you.*

"That's why good teams tend to do a lot of extreme stuff together," DeSteno says. "A constant stream of vulnerability gives them a much richer, more reliable estimate on what their trustworthiness is, and brings them closer, so they can take still more risks. It builds on itself."

The mechanism of cooperation can be summed up as follows: *Exchanges of vulnerability, which we naturally tend to avoid, are the pathway through which trusting cooperation is built.* This idea is useful because it gives us a glimpse inside the machinery of teamwork. Cooperation, as we'll see, does not simply descend out of the blue. It is a group muscle that is built according to a specific pattern of repeated interaction, and that pattern is always the same: a circle of people engaged in the risky, occasionally painful, ultimately rewarding process of being vulnerable together.

More immediately, the idea of vulnerability loops is useful because it helps illuminate connections between seemingly disparate worlds. For example, why are certain groups of comedians so successful? How is the world's most notorious band of jewel thieves structured? And what does carrying around a really heavy log have to do with creating the best Special Forces teams on the planet?

9 The Super-Cooperators

Draper Kauffman's Trust Machine

One of the traits that set Navy SEAL teams apart is their combination of stealth and adaptability. They can reliably navigate complex and dangerous landscapes in complete silence. This is one of the reasons SEALs are chosen to take on operations like the mission to kill Osama bin Laden, the mission to rescue Captain Richard Phillips on the *Maersk Alabama,* and thousands of lower-profile but equally risky missions. The SEALs call this combination of skills "playing pickup basketball." Like any good pickup team, they don't need to talk too much or follow some predetermined plan; they just play the game.

"We were once teamed on a mission with Rangers," one former Team Six commander told me, referring to the army's Special Forces teams. "The Rangers commander and I were together [at a nearby base] observing the [drone video] feed of the mission. The entire time the Ranger commander was on the radio with his guys. He was talking, giving orders—'Do this, look out for that.' He was acting like a coach on the sidelines yelling plays. At some point this commander notices I'm not saying a word, and he gives me this look, almost in disbelief. Like, *why aren't you telling your guys what to do?* It was pretty striking. Our guys and their guys, doing the same mission. He's talking the whole time, and we aren't saying a thing. And the answer is, *because we don't need to.* I know my guys are going to solve the problems themselves."

Within military circles, there are several theories on why the SEALs are skilled at playing pickup basketball. Some point to the rigors of the selection program, that steep pyramid of mental, emotional, and physical training from which only a small percentage of candidates emerge. Others point to the high quality of the individuals who are drawn to the unit, and to its relentless ethos of self-improvement.

All these theories make sense, but they do not suffice. Training for the army's Delta Force, for example, is equally difficult and even more selective. (It has a 95 percent dropout rate, as opposed to 67 percent for SEALs.) Other special operations groups draw high-quality individuals and center on relentless improvement. So why do SEAL teams work so well together? And as you dig for the answer, at some point you reach the story of a skinny, nearsighted, and titanically stubborn navy reject named Draper Kauffman.

Kauffman was born in 1911, the only son of the legendary navy admiral James "Stormy" Kauffman. He was what modern psychologists would term an oppositional child. He was keenly aware of what people wanted of him and tended to do the reverse. When he was five, he got in trouble for staying outside the house too late. "Hurry up and spank me so I can go back out and play," he told his mother. A mediocre student who was chided for laziness by his father, Kauffman graduated from the Naval Academy in 1933. When his poor eyesight prevented him from getting an officer's commission, he quit the military and took a job with a shipping company.

Then as World War II approached, he quit that job so he could volunteer as a driver for American Volunteer Ambulance Corps. His parents and sister, fearing for his safety, wrote letters asking him to reconsider. His response was to request a posting to the most dangerous place possible: the northern part of the Maginot Line, where Hitler had amassed his troops to invade France. Shortly after Kauffman arrived in February 1940, the war began.

Kauffman's first job was to drive the ambulance through the battlefield to pick up wounded. He was unprepared for the chaotic realities of battle. "I never would have done this if I'd known what it would be like," he wrote. "So many shells exploded in the road ahead . . . that my only instinct was to drive as fast as possible and I damn near wrecked the car doing it. After we got [the wounded] transferred to another ambulance to go back to the hospital, I sat in my driver's seat and started shaking like a leaf."

Around this time Kauffman encountered a group of French soldiers who represented everything he was not. The Corps Franc was an elite group of volunteers whose job was to sneak behind enemy lines, disrupt communication, take prisoners, and wreak havoc. They were organized in small teams, each carrying light arms and explosives. Kauffman was struck by their brotherly connection, which far exceeded anything he had encountered back at the Naval Academy. "You were either accepted by the Corps Franc or you weren't accepted, and the two were miles apart," he wrote his family. "There wasn't anything they wouldn't do for you. If one member of the patrol was trapped and there were five others, they would attack fifty Germans to try to free the one man who was trapped."

Over the course of six weeks, Kauffman spent days and nights with the Corps Franc, witnessing their nightly rituals of toasting the dead, and their cool under enemy fire. "You sincerely call a man a friend in a very short time when things are hot," he wrote. "This climaxed one day when I picked Toine [a member of the Corps] off the field with his face half gone, one arm shot to pieces, and his left foot gone. When we got him into the light of the Poste de Secours, I almost gave way, and he didn't help any by winking at me with his good eye and squeezing my hand with his good one."

After the Maginot Line was overrun, Kauffman traveled to Britain and volunteered with the bomb-disposal unit of the British Naval Reserves. In June 1943 he returned to the States and joined the Naval Reserve. Word spread about this skinny lieutenant with a talent for bomb disposal, and he was sent to Fort Pierce, Florida, assigned the task of selecting and training soldiers for underwater demolition units that would penetrate the German defenses along the French and North African coasts. The expectation was that Kauffman would follow the navy's template for training specialized teams: a few weeks of moderately strenuous selection and training, overseen by officers. Instead, he threw out the template and decided to re-create the Corps Franc.

First, Kauffman created Hell Week, a weeklong selection program filled with Maginot Line levels of pain, fear, and confusion, featuring four-mile open-water swims, obstacle courses, hand-to-hand combat training, ten-mile runs, paltry amounts of sleep, and a curious telephone-pole-lifting exercise he'd seen British commandos use to build strength and teamwork. Those who survived Hell Week (25 to 35 percent of the class) were given eight to ten weeks of specialized training where they learned and honed the more refined skills they would use in the field.

Second, Kauffman decreed that every aspect of the training be team-based. Instead of operating solo, trainees were put into groups of six (the number that fit in navy-issue rubber rafts) and kept together through the duration of training. What's more, each team had to be self-sufficient, able to navigate around or through any obstacle without relying on some central command.

Third, Kauffman eliminated the hierarchical distinction between officer and enlisted man. In his program, everyone did the training, no matter their rank. This, of course, included Kauffman. The enlisted men of the first class took one look at their ungainly, nearsighted commander and reached the same conclusion: There was no way this guy would make it. But as the trainees watched, he proved them wrong.

"We were testing [Kauffman] all along," wrote Dan Dillon, a member of the first demolition class, "but my respect for him deepened because a lot of officers will tell you what to do, but they won't do it themselves. This man . . . asks for suggestions. If they're good, he uses them. . . . And he participates in everything. . . . The dirtiest, rottenest jobs that we tackle, he is in there doing as well as the rest of us. How could you not respect him?"

The teams that graduated from Kauffman's makeshift training program were a success from the start, from Omaha Beach to the Pacific. In the 1960s, when President John Kennedy expanded the nation's unconventional warfare capabilities, Kauffman's training program was used as the template for what became the SEAL teams, and it remains so to this day. All of which adds up to an unusual situation: The world's most sophisticated and effective military teams are being built by an outdated, primitive, wholly unscientific program that hasn't changed in its essentials since the 1940s.

"I call it 'unconscious genius,'" one SEAL training officer tells me. "The people who built the original training program didn't completely understand *why* this was the best way to build teams, but they understood that it *was* the best way. It would be so easy now to go back and change things, to modernize them in some way. But we don't, because we appreciate the results."

If you go to SEAL training sites, you will find Draper Kauffman's telephone poles. They are stacked in the dunes near the SEAL obstacle courses in Coronado and Virginia Beach. They look like remnants from a construction project, but SEAL commanders consider them sacred objects. "Log PT [physical training] is the lens through which you can view everything that happens here," said Tom Freeman, a SEAL commander.* "It captures the essence of every evolution, because it's about teamwork."

Log PT is not complicated. Basically, it consists of six SEAL trainees performing an assortment of maneuvers that seem more appropriate to an Amish barn raising. They lift, carry, and roll the log. They move it from shoulder to shoulder and push it with their feet. They do sit-ups while cradling it, and they stand for long periods while holding it overhead with extended arms. There is no strategy, no technique, nothing that calls for higher levels of thought, skill, or reflection. What sets Log PT apart is its ability to deliver two conditions: intense vulnerability along with deep interconnectedness. Let's take them one by one.

First, vulnerability. In SEAL vernacular, you do not *do* Log PT. You *get* Log-PTed. In the vast storehouse of pain that comprises SEAL training, Log PT delivers some of the highest, purest levels of agony. "There are times when the instructors will tell you to be at the O-Course in thirty minutes, and that's when you realize: 'Holy shit, we're getting Log-PTed,'" Freeman says. "They send you to lunch first so you have time to fuel up and dread it. The worst part is the anticipation. You're thirty seconds into a ninety-minute evolution, and your shoulders are burning, and you're realizing that you've got an hour and a half more to go."

* Not his real name.

Second, interconnectedness. The weight (around 250 pounds) and length (ten feet) of the log lend it massive inertia; executing coordinated maneuvers requires each team member to apply the right amount of force at the right time, and the only way to do this is to pay keen attention to your teammates. Conceptually, it's like trying to twirl a baton with one hand: If your fingers and thumb work together with the proper timing, the task is simple; if the timing of one finger is off, even by a fraction of a second, it's impossible. That's why a physically weaker team that's working in sync can succeed in Log PT, while a bigger, stronger group can fall apart, physically and mentally.

These two conditions combine to deliver a highly particular sensation: the point where vulnerability meets interconnection. You are in immense pain, inches from your teammates, close enough to feel their breath on the back of your neck. When a teammate falters or makes a wrong move, you can feel it, and you know that they can feel it when you do the same. It adds up to a choice. You can focus on yourself, or you can focus on the team and the task.

When Log PT is done poorly, the log bucks and rolls, the trainees fight each other, and emotions rise. When Log PT is done well, it looks smooth and quiet. But that smoothness is an illusion, because just beneath the surface communication is happening. It takes the form of almost-invisible exchanges: Someone weakens, and the people next to him adjust their efforts to keep the log level and steady. Someone's grip slips, and the teammates instantly make up the difference. A conversation travels back and forth through the fibers of the log:

1. A teammate falters.
2. Others sense it, and respond by taking on more
   pain for the sake of the group.
3. Balance is regained.

Thanks to Draper Kauffman, this exchange of vulnerability and interconnection is woven into every aspect of SEAL training and enshrined in a set of iron values. Everything is done as a group. Trainees must keep track of one another at all times; there is no greater sin than losing track of someone. During boat exercises, trainees constantly trade positions and leadership roles. Timed performances on runs are supposed to be held to an unbreakable standard, but instructors have been known to bend those standards for runners who slow down in order to help others, because they value the willingness of one person taking a risk for the sake of the team.

"We're all about seeking the microevent," Freeman says. "Every evolution is a lens to look for teamwork moments, and we believe that if you stitch together a lot of opportunities, you start to know who the good teammates will be. It comes out at the oddest times. For instance, let's say they're running late and the instructors are going to hammer them. Does somebody just urge everyone to hurry up and take off running? Or do they stop and say, 'Look, we're gonna get hammered for being late anyway, so let's take a minute and get our gear tight, so when we show up we're a hundred percent ready.' There's something about that second guy that we want. We want to be with him because he's not thinking about himself; he's thinking of the team."

Seen in this way, the high level of cooperation among SEALs is not a surprise but closer to an inevitability. They cooperate well because Kauffman's training program generates thousands of microevents that build closeness and cooperation. "It's more than just teamwork," Freeman says. "You've left yourself wide open. Everybody on your team knows who you are, because you left it all on the table. And if you did well, it builds a level of trust that's exponentially higher than anything you can get anywhere else."

The Power of the Harold

One evening in 1999, Lorne Michaels, producer of *Saturday Night Live,* left his penthouse on West Sixty-ninth Street in New York and headed south to a run-down part of Chelsea. There he walked into a sixty-seat theater that, until a few months before, had been home to the Harmony Burlesque all-nude strip club. The air emanated mysterious smells; the Dumpster near the back entrance rustled with rats. In three years, city inspectors would shut the theater down for fire code violations. But this night Michaels was not paying attention to the setting. He had come to scout talent.

Michaels operated within the comedy ecosystem like an orchid collector: seeking, locating, and gathering the best species. In the past, he had located remarkable blooms of talent in his hometown of Toronto, in Chicago's Second City, at ImprovOlympic, and in other locales. But in recent months a new species of comedian had arrived: smart, fearless ensembles with high verbal IQ and a raunchy inventiveness. They were colonizing the entertainment landscape with breathtaking speed, the vanguard of an invasion that would star in and/or write for *The Office, The Daily Show, 30 Rock, The Colbert Report, Parks and Recreation, Community, Conan, Key & Peele, Broad City, Bob's Burgers, New Girl, The League, Girls,* and *Veep*—not to mention movies like *Anchorman, Talladega Nights, Bring it On,* and *Bridesmaids,* among others. They called themselves the Upright Citizens Brigade.*

The remarkable thing about the UCB, from Michaels's perspective, was their depth. While most other improv groups produced a small handful of great teams, UCB produced dozens, all of which could perform with remarkable skill. What's more, UCB didn't seem at first glance all that different from Second City or ImprovOlympic or any of the other comedy groups. All were influenced by the late comedy legend Del Close; all offered improv classes to create feeder systems of newcomers; all shared a boundary-breaking, anything-goes aesthetic. In fact, the only discernible difference was that UCB trained its comedians almost exclusively using a strange and difficult improv game called the Harold.

Most improv games are built on simplicity and speed—

---

* Here is a partial list of UCB alumni: Scott Adsit, Aziz Ansari, H. Jon Benjamin, Matt Besser, Kay Cannon, Rob Corddry, Eliza Coupe, Andrew Daly, Abby Elliott, Mary Elizabeth Ellis, Sue Galloway, Jon Glaser, Ilana Glazer, Donald Glover, Ed Helms, Rob Huebel, Abbi Jacobson, Jake Johnson, Ellie Kemper, Nick Kroll, John Lutz, Jason Mantzoukas, Jack McBrayer, Adam McKay, Kate McKinnon, Bobby Moynihan, Aubrey Plaza, Amy Poehler, June Diane Raphael, Rob Riggle, Ian Roberts, Horatio Sanz, Paul Scheer, Ben Schwartz, Jenny Slate, Jessica St. Clair, Matt Walsh, Tracey Wigfield, Jessica Williams, Casey Wilson, Zach Woods, and Sasheer Zamata.

creating brief sketches in response to audience prompts—but the Harold is different because it is long and complex. It requires eight people, contains nine interweaving scenes, and lasts around forty minutes—an eternity in the attention-deficit-disorder world of improv. The Harold is hard to teach and hard to learn, and as a result it often ends in spectacular failure. Del Close famously likened a successful Harold to watching a group of people tumble down the stairs at the same time and all land on their feet. The vast majority of the time, however, people just tumble down the stairs.

The structure of a Harold is as follows:

- Group Opening
- First Beat: Scenes 1A, 1B, 1C (two people each scene)
- Group Game
- Second Beat: Scenes 2A, 2B, 2C
- Group Game
- Third Beat: Scenes 3A, 3B, 3C

Don't worry if you can't follow it—in a way that's the point, because in a Harold you have to come up with interlinking scenes on the fly with seven other people; so that all the "A" scenes connect, all the "B" scenes connect, and so on. It requires you to pay deep attention to what the UCB calls "game," or the comic core of each scene, and to hold those threads in your mind, calling back previous connections as you build new ones.

Unlike other comedy groups, the UCB didn't perform Harolds once in a while. They were obsessed with Harolds.

There were Harold teams, Harold nights, Harold classes, Harold competitions, and Harold practices, as well as practices devoted to analyzing each element of the Harold. The walls of their theater were covered with photos of their best Harold teams. As one observer said, UCB's relationship to Harolds was roughly the same as the Catholic Church's relationship to celebrating Mass. All of which adds up to a curious situation: UCB was creating some of the most cohesive comic ensembles on the planet by spending a huge amount of time doing an activity that produced mostly pain and awkwardness.

To find out more, I go to a Harold Night at UCB's new (unsmelly and rat-free) theater on West Twenty-sixth Street in Chelsea. I find a seat and start chatting with my neighbor, a woman named Valerie, who like many in the audience is enrolled in UCB classes, hoping to make it onto a Harold team someday. She has come not to be entertained but to learn. "I'm watching for technique, mostly," she says. "How people respond under pressure. I'm really working on my reactions, trying to react to people in an authentic way and not with old habits."

The show begins: three teams, each of whom performs a Harold. After each Harold, Valerie offers a high-speed analysis. "Too closed off," she whispers after a Harold that involved a headphone-wearing woman on the subway singing an Adele song too loudly. "She didn't leave room for anybody else to connect. She was just making a joke, and there was nowhere for the others to go."

"Too straight," Valerie whispers after the second Harold, which involved a coffee machine that used its artificial intelligence to seduce its owner's girlfriend. She explains that a good Harold doesn't stay locked in the same story-space but allows players to make leaps to wildly different scenarios.

"That was amazing," Valerie whispers after the third Harold, which involved a vampire, a family on vacation, and a couple who gave birth to an animate sex toy. "They really supported each other. Did you see how some of them just let things play out without getting too involved? I love that."

When Del Close developed the Harold in the 1970s, he wrote down the following rules:

1. You are all supporting actors.
2. Always check your impulses.
3. Never enter a scene unless you are needed.
4. Save your fellow actor, don't worry about the piece.
5. Your prime responsibility is to support.
6. Work at the top of your brains at all times.
7. Never underestimate or condescend to the audience.
8. No jokes.
9. Trust. Trust your fellow actors to support you; trust them to come through if you lay something heavy on them; trust yourself.
10. Avoid judging what is going down except in terms of whether it needs help, what can best follow, or how you can support it imaginatively if your support is called for.
11. LISTEN.

Every rule directs you either to tamp down selfish instincts that might make you the center of attention, or to serve your fellow actors (*support, save, trust, listen*). This is why Close's rules are hard to follow, and also why they are useful in building cooperation. A Harold places you in front of an audience, then asks you to disobey every natural instinct in your brain and instead to give yourself selflessly to the group. In short, it's a comedy version of Log PT.

"You have to let go of the need to be funny, to be the center of things," says Nate Dern, former artistic director of UCB. "You have to be able to be naked, to be out of things to say, so that people can find things together. People say their minds should be blank, but that's not quite it. They should be open."

UCB is also unique in that it approaches Harolds as if they were a sport. This mentality is reflected in the terminology. There are coaches, not directors; practices, not rehearsals; and each Harold is followed by a rigorous feedback session much like an AAR or a BrainTrust meeting. "Some is positive, but mostly it's critique-based," Dern says. "Things like 'You didn't listen to your scene partner's idea.' Or 'You steamrollered your partner and didn't let them contribute.' It's pretty intense. As a performer, it's tough, because you already know you had a bad show, and then your coach will tell you all the things that were bad."

"In every other form of improv, you can get by on charm," says Kevin Hines, the academic supervisor of UCB New York. "Not in the Harold. It's totally unforgiving. Which is why the people who succeed here tend to be extremely hard workers."

In other words, the Harold is a group brain workout in which you experience, over and over, the pure, painful intersection of vulnerability and interconnection. Seen this way, UCB's brilliance on stage and screen is not an accident. It is the product of thousands of microevents, thousands of small interpersonal leaps that were made and supported. These groups are cohesive not because it's natural but because they've built, piece by piece, the shared mental muscles to connect and cooperate.

"They Think with One Brain"

Around 2000, the world's most exclusive jewelry stores began to be targeted by a new type of robber. These robbers operated in broad daylight, in the toniest shopping districts, in full view of security cameras. The method was usually the same: They entered the stores dressed as wealthy shoppers, then used hammers to smash the jewelry cases, taking only the most valuable gems. The robberies were well planned and well executed—most took fewer than forty-five seconds. Though the robbers were occasionally rough with guards and customers, they were averse to gunplay and creative in their escapes. In London, they departed in a chauffeured Bentley; in Tokyo, they used bicycles. One criminologist described their work as "artistry." The robbers were young, rumored to come from Serbia and Montenegro, parts of war-torn former Yugoslavia. Police called them the Pink Panthers.*

* The name originates from a 2003 London robbery where police discovered stolen diamonds hidden in a jar of face cream, a tactic made famous in the 1975 film *The Return of the Pink Panther*.

- Paris 2001: A group of Panthers posing as workmen used blowtorches to melt the security coating off the windows at the Paris-Boucheron flagship store, then smashed the windows and made off with jewels worth $1.5 million.
- Tokyo 2005: A group of Panthers posing as wealthy customers used pepper spray to disable security guards and left with jewels worth $35 million.
- St. Tropez 2005: Panthers dressed in sunhats and flowered shirts broke into a waterfront store, took $3 million worth of gems, and departed by speedboat.
- Dubai 2007: Four Panthers drove two rented Audis into the exclusive Wafi shopping mall and used the cars as battering rams to smash through the doorway of the Graff jewelry store. (They had disabled the cars' airbags so they didn't activate.) They left with jewels worth $3.4 million.
- London 2007: Four male Panthers dressed as middle-aged women, complete with wigs and expensive dresses, robbed a Harry Winston store and left with $105 million in emeralds, rubies, and diamonds the size of jelly beans.

When you view security camera footage of the robberies, the clips form a single, seamless loop. The Panthers move through the stores like water; their actions are coordinated, calm, and focused. They don't look at each other; they know where to go and what to do. They swing hammers at the

cases with calm precision, sweep away broken glass and ex-
tract the diamonds with practiced efficiency, then depart like
shadows.

Authorities were also impressed by something else: In a
line of work not known for loyalty, the Panthers seemed to
have a genuine attachment to one another. On rare occa-
sions when they were apprehended, they were immune to
police attempts to get them to turn state's evidence. In 2005,
a Panther named Dragan Mikic escaped from a French
prison when a group of men—presumably fellow Panthers—
used ladders, rifles, and wire cutters to break into the prison
and free him. As one prosecutor said, "These guys don't
care about being put in jail. They know they are going to
escape." As another observer put it, "They think with one
brain."

As the Panthers' notoriety increased, people wondered
who they were and how they were organized. The most gen-
erally accepted theory was that they consisted of a group of
former soldiers who'd served in the Yugoslavian wars. Some
believed the Panthers to be former members of a paramili-
tary unit called Arkan's Tigers, an infamous group who
worked for strongman Slobodan Milosevic. Others believed
them to be former members of the JSO, Serbian special
forces.

Wherever they came from, there seemed no question that
they were soldiers commanded and controlled by some central figure. As George Papasifakis, deputy of the Greek
Property Crimes Unit, told a reporter, "Someone is definitely
moving the strings on the ground in Serbia, and someone is

in charge of initiating and educating the younger members."
It's thrilling, cinematic stuff: a secret global organization of
ex-commandos-turned-supercriminals, summoned to their
missions by a shadowy leader. This narrative makes sense
because we tend to presume that such faultless coordination
requires special training, powerful leadership, and central-
ized organization.

It is a perfectly good theory, but it has one problem: It
is wrong. In the latter part of the decade, the investigative
efforts of police and journalists gradually revealed the surprising truth. The Panthers were a self-assembling, self-
governing, free-range mix of middle-class people, former
athletes, and small-time criminals. One had been a member
of Serbia's national youth basketball team. Another had attended law school. What they had in common was the experience of living through a hellish war, an instinct for action,
strong friendships, and the realization that they had nothing
to lose.

"Most of them grew up together in three particular towns,
as friends," says director Havana Marking, who helped un-
cover the story in her documentary *Smash & Grab*. "The
experience of going through the communist regime and then
the free-for-all nightmare of the war that followed, that really bonded them. They were mostly smugglers at the beginning, to survive. They worked together in those environments,
and it wasn't for money, it was for survival. They learned
how to fake documents and cross borders, as well as other
skills. They were attracted to adrenaline and action. You
have to understand that crime, in the Balkans, was a normal
life. If what happened in the Balkans hadn't happened, these

people probably would have been entrepreneurs, lawyers, and journalists."

Each team was built around a set of well-defined roles. There was a *zavodnik,* a "seducer" who scouts the location (usually a woman); a *magare,* or muscle for getting the jewels; a *jatak,* who arranged logistics. While there were leaders on each team, they did not issue orders. Instead, they operated according to a simple rule that one Panther explained to Marking: "We all depend on each other."

This interdependence began with the way the Panthers prepared for each robbery. Each team member (there were never more than five or six on a team) moved to the city and gathered information on the target store. They lived and worked together for weeks of intensive planning. They scouted the store, tracked the comings and goings of the employees, and sketched maps of the layout to target the most valuable gems. What's more, each Panther shared the cost of the planning (which was not insignificant: the advance costs for the Tokyo robbery were $100,000). They did not rely on any outside structure or safety net. They *were* the structure, and if any of them failed, the group would fail.

In other words, the Panthers were a little bit like comedians doing a Harold, or SEALs doing Log PT—small teams solving problems in a constant state of vulnerability and interconnection. As one Panther named Lela told Marking, "My one mistake would be their fall. If I make an error somewhere, they are doomed."

For her film, Marking interviewed a man and woman who were formerly on the same Panther team but hadn't seen each other in some years. She watched how they interacted. "They hadn't seen each other for a long time, and they were really happy to see each other," she says. "They had a proper friendship and seemed to be genuinely close. You know how you can sense when two people are completely relaxed in each other's company? You could sense it with them."

How to Create Cooperation in Small Groups

Dave Cooper's Rules

If you were to seek out the highest-performing teams on the planet, at some point you would find yourself in Dam Neck, Virginia, home base for Draper Kauffman's descendants: the three hundred Navy SEALs who make up Team Six. And if you were to ask a variety of current and retired Team Six operators which leaders they admire most, you would hear the same handful of names over and over. But the name you would hear most often is Dave Cooper.

This is a surprising choice, because Dave Cooper does not possess any obvious talents that distinguish him from the rest of Team Six. Cooper, who retired in 2012, is neither the smartest nor the strongest team member, nor the best marksman. He is not the best swimmer nor the best at close quarters combat. But he happens to be the best at a skill that is at once hard to define and immensely valuable. He's the best at creating great teams.

"Coop is a very intelligent guy who stayed in the trenches for a long time," says former Team Six operator Christopher Baldwin. "He wasn't one of those people who moved up the leadership chain just to move up. He's one of us. He understood the bigger picture, and you could always talk to him."

"There are some higher-ups who've had run-ins with him, and he doesn't always follow the rules," says another operator. "But if you're on his team, you can see why he's effective."

Another operator puts it more succinctly: "Cooper is the dude."

They tell me how Cooper worked in Bosnia, Somalia, Iraq, and Afghanistan, always in places that were "sporty," to use the SEAL term. They tell me how well Cooper's teams worked together, and how often they succeeded when things went to hell—especially when they went to hell. The more they talk, the more Cooper expands in my imagination to become a larger-than-life figure, a combination of Vince Lombardi and Jason Bourne.

Then at a restaurant in Virginia Beach, we meet for lunch.

Cooper turns out to be a medium-size guy in a beach shirt, shorts, and flip-flops who in most aspects resembles a suburban dad. As you might expect, he is extremely fit. As you might not expect, he is chatty and warm, with eyebrows that steeple together in concern when he listens. Like most SEAL operators, he carries himself with his elbows slightly away from his body, radiating awareness, scanning the room. Controlling the space, this is called.

He picks an outside table, so we can see the crowd. He chats with the waiter, listening to the specials with warm intensity. Then the eyebrows steeple. "So, what do you want to know?" he asks.

Cooper's backstory, like that of most Team Six guys, is idiosyncratic. He was raised in small-town Pennsylvania and grew up wanting to be a doctor. He majored in molecular biology at Juniata College, a tiny liberal arts school that allowed military recruiters on campus just one day a year. He heard of the SEALs from a history teacher and could still recite the line that hooked him: "SEALs are highly intelligent, copious readers." He was fascinated, and after graduation, he made his way to training. He survived Hell Week, passed Draper Kauffman's selection process, and made it through another selection to join Team Six in 1993.

There are many stories Cooper can tell—and many he cannot—about life as a Team Six operator. But when you ask him about building teams, he tells only one story. It happened in Afghanistan on New Year's Eve 2001, on a desolate road between Bagram and Jalalabad. Cooper was on that road because he had received an order to accompany his commander on a four-person route-reconnaissance mission in which they would drive from Bagram to Jalalabad and back in a single day.

The road was a nightmare: an explosive-infested, often impassable 110-mile stretch populated by bandits and insurgents. But Cooper's commander insisted they go, exuding confidence as he outlined the plan: They would ride in an armored Suburban with specially reinforced tires. They would be fast and stealthy. Everything would be fine. Cooper held his doubts, followed rank, and went along.

From the first miles out of Bagram, things started to go sideways. The road turned out to be worse than expected—in places more like a hiking trail than a highway. The ground clearance on the armored Suburban was only a few inches, so they were slowed to a crawl much of the time. By nightfall, when they finally reached Jalalabad, Cooper figured they would stay and wait for daylight. Instead, the commander announced they would be turning around and driving back to Bagram that night so they could complete the mission as planned.

Cooper objected—that was a bad idea, he said. The discussion got heated; Cooper and his commander yelled back and forth before the commander finally invoked his rank. Cooper submitted. With a sinking feeling, he climbed in the Suburban, and the group set off into the night.

The ambush happened an hour later. A convoy of trucks and jeeps rumbled out of the blackness and surrounded the Suburban. Cooper's driver tried to escape, but the reinforced tires blew out. They were driving on rims, in the dark, with gunfire arriving from all directions. One SEAL operator was bleeding, shot through the leg. It was, as Cooper says, an unmitigated shit show.

The SEALs had no choice but to surrender, climbing out with their arms raised, sure they were about to be killed. "For some reason, they decided not to shoot us," Cooper says. "Either they were scared of retaliation, or they saw that we weren't much of a threat." The insurgents roared off into the darkness, carrying the SEALs' weapons. Cooper and his team were able to contact Delta and British Special Forces units, which flew in to rescue them a few hours later. He returned to Bagram with a second chance and a new worldview.

"That night put me on a different path," Cooper says. "From that moment on, I realized that I needed to figure out ways to help the group function more effectively. The problem here is that, as humans, we have an authority bias that's incredibly strong and unconscious—if a superior tells you to do something, by God we tend to follow it, even when it's wrong. Having one person tell other people what to do is not a reliable way to make good decisions. So how do you create conditions where that doesn't happen, where you develop a hive mind? How do you develop ways to challenge each other, ask the right questions, and never defer to authority? We're trying to create leaders among leaders. And you can't just tell people to do that. You have to create the conditions where they start to do it."

Starting that night in 2001, Cooper set out to build those conditions for his teams. His approach to nurturing cooperation could be described as an insurgent campaign against authority bias. Merely creating space for cooperation, he realized, wasn't enough; he had to generate a series of unmistakable signals that tipped his men away from their natural tendencies and toward interdependence and cooperation. "Human nature is constantly working against us," he says. "You have to get around those barriers, and they never go away."

He started with small things. A new team member who called him by his title was quickly corrected: "You can call me Coop, Dave, or Fuckface, it's your choice." When Cooper gave his opinion, he was careful to attach phrases that provided a platform for someone to question him, like "Now let's see if someone can poke holes in this" or "Tell me what's wrong with this idea." He steered away from giving orders and instead asked a lot of questions. *Anybody have any ideas?*

During missions, Cooper sought opportunities to spotlight the need for his men to speak up, especially with newer team members. He was not subtle. "For example, when you're in an urban environment, windows are bad," he tells me. "You stand in front of one, and you can get shot by a sniper and never know where it came from. So if you're a new guy and you see me standing in front of a window in Fallujah, what are you going to say? Are you going to tell me to move my ass, or are you going to stand there quietly and let me get shot? When I ask new guys that question, they say, 'I'll tell you to move.' So I tell them, 'Well, that's exactly how you should conduct yourself all the time around here, with every single decision.'"

Cooper began to develop tools. "There're things you can do," he says. "Spending time together outside, hanging out—those help. One of the best things I've found to improve a team's cohesion is to send them to do some hard, hard training. There's something about hanging off a cliff together, and being wet and cold and miserable together, that makes a team come together."

One of the most useful tools was the After-Action Review, the truth-telling session we referenced in Chapter 7. AARs happen immediately after each mission and consist of a short meeting in which the team gathers to discuss and replay key decisions. AARs are led not by commanders but by enlisted men. There are no agendas, and no minutes are kept. The goal is to create a flat landscape without rank, where people can figure out what really happened and talk about mistakes—especially their own.

"It's got to be safe to talk," Cooper says. "Rank switched

off, humility switched on. You're looking for that moment where people can say, 'I screwed that up.' In fact, I'd say those might be the most important four words any leader can say: *I screwed that up*."

Good AARs follow a template. "You have to do it right away," Cooper says. "You put down your gun, circle up, and start talking. Usually you take the mission from beginning to end, chronologically. You talk about every decision, and you talk about the process. You have to resist the temptation to wrap it all up in a bow, and try to dig for the truth of what happened, so people can really learn from it. You have to ask why, and then when they respond, you ask another why. Why did you shoot at that particular point? What did you see? How did you know? What other options were there? You ask and ask and ask."

The goal of an AAR is not to excavate truth for truth's sake, or to assign credit and blame, but rather to build a shared mental model that can be applied to future missions. "Look, nobody can see it all or know it all," Cooper says. "But if you keep getting together and digging out what happened, then after a while everybody can see what's really happening, not just their small piece of it. People can share experiences and mistakes. They can see how what they do affects others, and we can start to create a group mind where everybody can work together and perform to the team's potential."

Cooper uses the phrase "backbone of humility" to describe the tone of a good AAR. It's a useful phrase because it captures the paradoxical nature of the task: a relentless willingness to see the truth and take ownership. With an

AAR, as with Log PT or a Harold, group members have to combine discipline with openness. And as with a Log PT or a Harold, it's not easy. But it does pay off.

After his revelation on the road to Bagram, Cooper spent the next decade leading teams, mostly in the Middle East. He gradually rose to Team Six's highest enlisted rank of command master chief, which placed him in charge of the entire group's training. In March 2011 he and another Team Six leader were summoned by Admiral William McRaven, commander of Joint Special Operations Command, to CIA headquarters in McLean, Virginia.

McRaven got right to the point: "We think we've found Osama bin Laden." He then outlined the plan. Team Six operators would fly into Pakistan in stealth helicopters, fast-rope onto the compound's roof, and kill the Al Qaeda leader.

Cooper listened, his attention drawn to one element: the stealth helicopters. He knew they were attractive to McRaven because they were invisible to radar and would thus allow the team to travel undetected through Pakistani airspace. But Cooper also knew they were untested in combat, and that special ops history was littered with disasters caused by using untested tools in combat. So he spoke up.

"With all due respect, sir," Cooper said, "I would not use those helicopters on this mission. I would plan something else in parallel. If we can't go with something else, then I go with the helicopters."

"We're not changing the plan now," McRaven said.

Cooper decided to keep pushing. He wanted to get this on the table. "Sir, I'd be remiss if I didn't tell you what I thought."

McRaven raised his voice. "We're not changing the plan now," he said.

"In that moment, I was pretty sure I was getting fired," Cooper tells me later. "But I wasn't going to keep my mouth shut." He pushed again.

McRaven shut him down again. The discussion was over.

Cooper walked out of that room facing a problem: How do you follow an order that carries what you consider to be an unacceptably high risk? In essence, he was in precisely the same position he'd been in back on the road to Bagram on New Year's Eve 2001. Should he follow the order or defy it?

Cooper chose a third path. He accepted the use of the stealth helicopters and also started preparing in case they failed. In the ensuing weeks, the SEALs built replicas of Bin Laden's compound in North Carolina, Nevada, and Afghanistan. In each place, Cooper ran downed-helicopter scenarios over and over. He simulated crashes outside the compound, inside the compound, on the roof, in the yard, hundreds of yards away. Each was essentially the same: Partway through the operation, Cooper would surprise the team with the order "You're going down, now." The pilots would autorotate the helicopter to the ground, and the team would then attack the mock compound from wherever they happened to be. "There were never any right or wrong answers; they had to self-organize and deal with the problem," Cooper said. "Then we'd do an AAR, talk about it, and figure out what had happened and what we could do better next time."

The downed-helicopter drills were not easy. They demanded a high level of attention, cooperation, and improvisation. In the AARs that followed each drill, the team members repeatedly went over what went wrong, owned mistakes, and talked about how they might do it better. "We ran so many that it became a joke among the guys," Cooper says. "They were saying, 'Hey, Coop, can we *please* run another downed-helicopter scenario?'"

On May 1, the White House sent the order to launch. The two stealth helicopters lifted off from the U.S. air base in Jalalabad. At the base's command center, Cooper, McRaven, and other commanders gathered around the screen to watch the drone video feed. In the White House, President Barack Obama and his national security team leaned in, watching the same images.

The mission started smoothly. They made it through Pakistani airspace undetected and approached Bin Laden's compound. But as the first helicopter attempted to land, things went wrong. One helicopter skidded around in the air as if it were on ice, veering and spinning toward the ground. The other helicopter, which was supposed to land on the roof of the main compound, saw the problems and veered off to land outside. (The explanation that later emerged was that the high walls of the compound created downdrafts that disrupted flight. The rehearsals had all been done at mockup compounds with chain-link fence, not solid walls.) Then things got worse. The first pilot, unable to keep altitude, crash-landed in the courtyard, lodging the tail section on the wall and tipping the helicopter on its side, burying its nose in the soft dirt. In the command post, the generals stared wordlessly at the screen. For three or four seconds, the room filled with an unbearable silence.

Then they saw it: Team Six operators pouring out of the downed helicopter, just as they had in the drills, going to work. They got moving and started working the problem—pickup basketball at its finest. "They didn't miss a beat," Cooper says. "Once they got on the ground, there was zero doubt." Thirty-eight minutes later, it was over, and the entire planet had an opportunity to appreciate the team's skill and bravery. But in all the celebration, it's easy to miss the deeper skill, the chain of training and AARs that laid the foundation for that moment.

From afar, the Bin Laden raid looked like a demonstration of team strength, power, and control. But that strength was built of a willingness to spot and confront the truth and to come together to ask a simple question over and over: *What's really going on here?* Cooper and his team did not have to go back again and again to work on downed-helicopter scenarios. But they succeeded because they understood that being vulnerable together is the only way a team can become invulnerable.

"When we talk about courage, we think it's going against an enemy with a machine gun," Cooper says. "The real courage is seeing the truth and speaking the truth to each other. People never want to be the person who says, 'Wait a second, what's really going on here?' But inside the squadron, that *is* the culture, and that's why we're successful."

11 How to Create Cooperation with Individuals

The Nyquist Method

Back in the early part of the last century, well before Silicon Valley, the world's foremost hub of invention and innovation was located in a series of large nondescript buildings in suburban New Jersey. It was called Bell Labs. Originally formed in 1925 to help build a national communications network, Bell Labs grew into the scientific equivalent of Renaissance-era Florence: a wellspring of group genius that lasted until the 1970s. Led by Claude Shannon, a brilliant polymath who liked to ride through the halls on his unicycle while juggling, Bell Labs and its teams of scientists invented and developed the transistor, data networking, solar cells, lasers, communications satellites, binary computing, and cellular communication—in short, most of the tools we use to live modern life.

Midway through that golden age, some Bell Labs administrators grew curious about the reasons for their own remarkable success. They wondered which Bell scientists had generated the most patents for their inventions, and whether those scientists had anything in common. They began by examining the Bell patent library, where patents were kept in binders organized alphabetically by the scientists' last name.

"Most of the binders were about the same size," recalls Bill Keefauver, a lawyer who worked in the patent office. "But some binders stood out right away because they were fat—much fatter than everyone else's. Those were the super-creative people who had filed dozens and dozens of patents. There were about ten of them."

The administrators studied those ten scientists, hunting for the common thread. Did the supercreatives share the same specialty? The same educational background? The same family background? After considering and discarding dozens of possible ties, they discovered a connection—and it didn't have to do with who the supercreatives were. It had to do with a habit that they shared: the habit of regularly eating lunch in the Bell Labs cafeteria with a quiet Swedish engineer named Harry Nyquist.

This result came as a surprise, to say the least. Not because Nyquist wasn't well known—he was, having pioneered important advances in telegraphy and feedback amplification. But in a place famous for its dynamic and eccentric leaders, Nyquist was the opposite: a mild, gently smiling Lutheran known mostly for his tranquil reliability. Raised on a Swedish farm, he approached his work with old-world discipline. He awoke at precisely 6:45 each morning, departed for the office at precisely 7:30, and was always home for family dinner at 6:15. His most idiosyncratic habit was occasionally taking the ferry instead of the subway on his commute home. (He enjoyed the fresh air.) He was so ordinary as to be nearly invisible. In other words, the most important person in one of the most creative places in history turned out to be the person almost everyone would overlook. Which is why it's important to look a bit more closely at his skill set.

Nyquist by all accounts possessed two important qualities. The first was warmth. He had a knack for making people feel cared for; every contemporary description paints him as "fatherly." The second quality was a relentless curiosity. In a landscape made up of diverse scientific domains, he combined breadth and depth of knowledge with a desire to seek connections. "Nyquist was full of ideas, full of questions," Bell Labs engineer Chapin Cutler recalls. "He drew people out, got them thinking."

"Nyquist was good at a particular kind of activity that Bell really encouraged in those days," Keefauver says. "People in all kinds of disciplines, on all kinds of projects, talking about their project with someone who's working on something entirely different, to put a new light on things. People like Harry Nyquist could capture what someone was doing, throw some new ideas at them, and ask, 'Why don't you try that?'"

When I visited groups for this book, I met a lot of people who possessed traits of warmth and curiosity—so many, in fact, that I began to think of them as Nyquists. They were polite, reserved, and skilled listeners. They radiated a safe, nurturing vibe. They possessed deep knowledge that spanned domains and had a knack for asking questions that ignited motivation and ideas. (The best way to find the Nyquist is usually to ask people: *If I could get a sense of the way your culture works by meeting just one person, who would that person be?*) If we think of successful cultures as engines of human cooperation, then the Nyquists are the spark plugs.

The person I met who best embodied this process was named Roshi Givechi.

Roshi Givechi works at the New York office of IDEO, the international design firm headquartered in Palo Alto, California. IDEO's place in the modern world is a little like that of Bell Labs. It has designed, among other things, the original Apple computer mouse, insulin pens for diabetics, and the standup toothpaste tube. It has won more design awards than any other company in history. The group consists of six hundred people who are divided into small teams and tasked with meeting challenges that range from designing global plans for disaster response to building a smartphone-charging handbag and everything in between.

Officially, Givechi is a designer. Unofficially, her role is to serve as roving catalyst, involved in a number of projects, helping the teams navigate the design process. "When teams are stuck, or if there's a tough dynamic, Roshi is like magic," says Duane Bray, an IDEO partner. "She's incredibly skilled at unlocking teams, asking questions that connect people and open possibilities. The truth is, we don't quite understand how she does it, exactly. We just know that it works really well."

Givechi, a small woman in her forties, wears flowing skirts with large pockets. She has dark, curly hair and quick, dark eyes with smile-crinkles at the corners. On greeting, she makes no attempt to charm—no jokes, no extended small talk. She projects none of the energetic theatricality you encounter with many people in creative work. Instead, she radiates a contented stillness, as if you've met many times before.

"Socially, I'm not the chattiest person," Givechi says. "I love stories, but I'm not the person in the middle of the room telling the story. I'm the person on the side listening and asking questions. They're usually questions that might seem obvious or simple or unnecessary. But I love asking them because I'm trying to understand what's really going on."

Givechi's interactions with her teams take place largely in what IDEO calls Flights, regular all-team meetings that occur at the start, middle, and finish of every project. (Think of them as IDEO's version of the BrainTrust or AAR.) Givechi approaches each Flight from the outside in. She does her research, mostly through conversations, to learn the issues the team has been wrestling with, both from a design perspective (what are the barriers?) and from a team-dynamics perspective (where is the friction?). Then with that landscape in mind, she gathers the group and asks questions designed to unearth tensions and help the group gain clarity about themselves and the project. The word she uses for this process is *surfacing.*

"I like the word *connect*," Givechi says. "For me, every conversation is the same, because it's about helping people

---

* Halfway through our conversation, Givechi asked me about this book's title and subtitle. I told her, and she paused—a long, meaningful pause. Then she asked, "Does that subtitle really work?" A few minutes later, after a few back-and-forths, this book had a new and improved subtitle. I'm not certain if I suggested the change or if she did. As Givechi would say, we surfaced it together.

walk away with a greater sense of awareness, excitement, and motivation to make an impact. Because individuals are really different. So you have to find different ways to make it comfortable and engaging for people to share what they're really thinking about. It's not about decisiveness—it's about discovery. For me, that has to do with asking the right questions the right way."*

When you talk to Givechi's colleagues, they point out a paradox: She is at once soft and hard, empathetic but also persistent. "There's an underlying toughness to Roshi," says Lawrence Abrahamson, an IDEO design director. "She doesn't present an agenda, but of course there is an agenda behind that, and it's gentle guiding. And one of the biggest tools in her toolbox is time. She'll spend so much time, being patient and continuing to have conversations and making sure the conversations are progressing in a good direction."

"There's always a moment with Roshi," says Peter Antonelli, a design director. "There's a spirit of provocation constantly at play, to nudge, to help us think beyond what's immediately in front of us. And it usually starts with questioning the big obvious things. It's never confrontational—she never says, 'You're doing the wrong thing.' It's organic, embedded in conversation."

Watching Givechi listen is like watching a skilled athlete in action. She listens chiefly with her eyes, which have a Geiger-counter-like sensitivity to changes in mood and expression. She detects small changes and responds to them

---

* Robert Bales, one of the first scientists to study group communication, discovered that while questions comprise only 6 percent of verbal interactions, they generate 60 percent of ensuing discussions.

swiftly. If you convey a scintilla of tension about a subject, she will mark it and follow up with a question designed to gently explore the reasons for that tension. When she speaks, she constantly links back to you with small phrases—*Maybe you've had an experience like this . . . Your work might be similar . . . The reason I was pausing there was . . .* —that provide a steady signal of connection. You find yourself comfortable opening up, taking risks, telling the truth.

It feels like magic, but in fact it's the result of a lot of practice. As a child, Givechi would use a cassette recorder to capture her voice reading her favorite books over and over, fascinated by the way tiny shifts in tone and timing could transform meaning. As a college student, studying psychology and design, she volunteered to assist the blind, and she wrote her college thesis on dance and choreography. She uses the idea of dance to describe the skills she employs with IDEO's design teams: to find the music, support her partner, and follow the rhythm. "I don't see myself as the conductor of the music," she says. "I'm more of a nudger. I nudge the choreography and try to create the conditions for good things to happen."

A year ago IDEO decided to scale Givechi's abilities across the organization. They asked her to create modules of questions teams could ask themselves, then provided those modules to design teams as tools to help them improve. For example, here are a few:

- The one thing that excites me about this particular opportunity is _____

- I confess, the one thing I'm not so excited about
  with this particular opportunity is _____
- On this project, I'd really like to get better at
  _____

The interesting thing about Givechi's questions is how transcendently simple they are. They have less to do with design than with connecting to deeper emotions: fear, ambition, motivation. It's easy to imagine that in different hands, these questions could fall flat and fail to ignite conversation. This is because the real power of the interaction is located in the two-way emotional signaling that creates an atmosphere of connection that surrounds the conversation.

"The word *subtle* is the key," says Abrahamson. "She's unassuming and disarms people because she is so open and listening and caring. Roshi has the ability to pause completely, to stop what must be going on in her head, to focus completely on the person and the question at hand, and to see where that question is leading. She isn't trying to drag you somewhere, ever. She's truly seeing you from your position, and that's her power."

"The word *empathy* sounds so soft and nice, but that's not what's really going on," says Njoki Gitahi, a senior communication designer. "What Roshi does requires a critical understanding of what makes people tick, and what makes people tick isn't always being nice to them. Part of it is that she knows people so well that she understands what they need. Sometimes what they need is support and praise. But sometimes what they need is a little knock on the chin, a reminder that they need to work harder, a nudge to try new things. That's what she gives."

"She's really listening, hearing what you said and asking what it means, digging deeper," says Nili Metuki, design researcher. "She doesn't let things stay unclear, even when they're uncomfortable. Especially when they're uncomfortable."

Whereupon we must ask: What is inside that pause, that Nyquistian moment of vulnerable, authentic connection? That is, can we peer inside this moment and see what's really happening underneath?

That's a question Dr. Carl Marci has spent much of his career exploring. Marci, a neurologist who teaches at Harvard, first became fascinated with listening in a medical school class that featured a series of non-Western healers. These healers were unconventional, employing a spectacular range of methods that were scientifically dubious—for example, giving massage where the hands didn't touch the patient, or administering drops of water with concentrations of ingredients that approached zero—and yet they achieved remarkable results. One reason, Marci came to see, was the connection the healer formed with the patient.

"What these healers all had in common was that they were brilliant listeners. They would sit down, take a long patient history, and really get to know their patients," Marci says. "They were all incredibly empathic people who were really good at connecting with people and forming trusting bonds. So that's when I realized that the interesting part wasn't the healing but the listening, and the relationship being formed. That's what we needed to study."

Marci invented a method in which he videoed conversations while tracking galvanic skin response—the change in electrical resistance that measures emotional arousal. He discovered that for much of the time, the arousal curves of two people in conversation bore little or no relation to each other. But he also found special moments, in certain conversations, when the two curves fell into perfect sync. Marci called these moments concordances.

"Concordances happen when one person can react in an authentic way to the emotion being projected in the room," Marci says. "It's about understanding in an empathic way, then doing something in terms of gesture, comment, or expression that creates a connection."

One of the concordance videos included Marci himself. He is seated in a chair facing an older man in a gray three-piece suit, who happens to be his therapist. Marci is describing the day he proposed to his then-girlfriend. The machine sits between them, capturing the fluctuations of the inner landscape and projecting them onto the screen in the form of a pair of brightly colored, shifting lines: blue for Marci, and green for the man in the gray suit.

MARCI: We like to go to Bread and Circus and get their vegetable samosas. I said, "Well, I'll treat, we'll get some of those." So she figured we were going to have a picnic up there or something.
GRAY SUIT: [series of small, affirming nods]
MARCI: The second thought she had was maybe, we'll occasionally go up there and watch the sunset, she said maybe there was something funky going on in the sky.

GRAY SUIT: [big, definitive nod]

MARCI: And she said literally, for like a nanosecond, she entertained the idea that I was going to propose, but [the idea] went out faster than it went in.

GRAY SUIT: [sympathetic nod, head tilt]

MARCI: So she gets up there and she's all dressed, looking stunning as she always does, and she says, "What's up?" In hindsight she was looking for food and couldn't find it.

GRAY SUIT: [small smile.]

MARCI: I said, "Come sit." I recited the first stanza of the e. e. cummings poem, and it goes, "Being to time-lessness as it's to time, love did no more begin than love will end."

GRAY SUIT: [head tilts upward, eyebrows up]

MARCI (continuing to quote): "Where nothing is to breathe to stroll to swim, love is the air the ocean and the land." And I said, "You are my air, and my ocean, and my land."

GRAY SUIT: [head tilt, smile, nod]

MARCI: And it was just the most touching thing, because she realized what I was doing as I got the ring out, and just wept in a way that was so sincere and so earnest, and she was so overwhelmed. It was touch-ing. It was nice. She was psyched.

GRAY SUIT: [small, affirming nods]

Watching the video, the first thing you notice is that the conversation contains several moments of perfect concor-dance, where the green and blue lines move with a perfect coordination, rising and falling like pennants rippling in a breeze. The second thing you notice is that these moments happen without Gray Suit ever speaking a word. That is not to say that Gray Suit is not interacting. He radiates a steady attention, a poised stillness. His hands are folded on his lap. His eyes are up and alert. He reacts with nods, small expressions. In other words, he is doing what Roshi Givechi does at IDEO, and what Harry Nyquist presumably did at Bell Labs. He is demonstrating that the most important moments in conversation happen when one person is actively, intently listening.

"It's not an accident that concordance happens when there's one person talking and the other person listening," Marci says. "It's very hard to be empathic when you're talking. Talking is really complicated, because you're thinking and planning what you're going to say, and you tend to get stuck in your own head. But not when you're listening. When you're really listening, you lose time. There's no sense of yourself, because it's not about you. It's all about this task—to connect completely to that person."

Marci has connected increases in concordances to increases in perceived empathy: the more concordances occur, the closer the two people feel. What's more, the changes in closeness happen not gradually but all at once. "There's often one moment where it happens," he says. "There's an accelerated change to the relationship that happens when you're able to really listen, to be incredibly present with the person. It's like a breakthrough—'We were like this, but now we're going to interact in a new way, and we both understand that it's happened.'"

12 Ideas for Action

Building habits of group vulnerability is like building a muscle. It takes time, repetition, and the willingness to feel pain in order to achieve gains. And as with building muscle, the first key is to approach the process with a plan. With that in mind, here are a few workout ideas, for both individuals and groups.

Make Sure the Leader Is Vulnerable First and Often: As we've seen, group cooperation is created by small, frequently repeated moments of vulnerability. Of these, none carries more power than the moment when a leader signals vulnerability. As Dave Cooper says, *I screwed that up* are the most important words any leader can say.

I saw a vivid example when I watched restaurateur Danny Meyer run one of his morning meetings with his staff (about twenty people). Meyer, whom we'll meet up close in Chapter 15, is the founder of Union Square Cafe, Shake Shack, Gramercy Tavern, and a number of other restaurants that together are worth more than a billion dollars. The night before my visit, he had delivered his first-ever TED Talk. The staff meeting began with the group watching a video of Meyer's speech. Then the lights went up, and Meyer spoke.

"Can you see my leg shaking?" he asked the group. "I was so nervous, I was shaking like a leaf. I've given a lot of speeches, but the TED people wanted something more, something deeper and thoughtful. So I slept about three hours the night before, which is why I have those bags under my eyes. We had a terrible rehearsal, and I kept screwing up the PowerPoint. So it was almost a complete shit show. Except that I'm lucky enough to have some absolutely brilliant help." He paused and pointed. "Thanks, Chip and Haley. They made the whole thing work. They wrote great stuff, gave me great advice, and kept me together." Everyone looked at Chip and Haley and gave a short round of applause while Meyer looked on approvingly.

Meyer delivered the message—*I was scared*—with steadiness, confidence, and comfort that underlined the deeper message: *It's safe to tell the truth here*. His vulnerability isn't weakness; it's his strength.

Laszlo Bock, former head of People Analytics at Google, recommends that leaders ask their people three questions:

- What is one thing that I currently do that you'd like me to continue to do?
- What is one thing that I don't currently do frequently enough that you think I should do more often?
- What can I do to make you more effective?

"The key is to ask not for five or ten things but just one," Bock says. "That way it's easier for people to answer. And when a leader asks for feedback in this way, it makes it safe for the people who work with them to do the same. It can get contagious."

Overcommunicate Expectations: The successful groups I visited did not presume that cooperation would happen on its own. Instead, they were explicit and persistent about sending big, clear signals that established those expectations, modeled cooperation, and aligned language and roles to maximize helping behavior. IDEO is a good example. Its leaders constantly talk about the expectation of cooperation. (CEO Tim Brown incessantly repeats his mantra that the more complex the problem, the more help you need to solve it.) They clearly define helping roles and model vulnerability. (Their internal bulletin boards are filled with requests: *Does anybody know of a good yoga class? Can anybody help me find a cat sitter for Christmas week?*) In case you miss those signals, they are also written in big letters both on the walls of the New York office and in the pages of the *Little Book of IDEO,* a copy of which is given to every employee. Among the refrains: *Collaborate* and *Make Others Successful: Going Out of Your Way to Help Others Is the Secret Sauce.*

Deliver the Negative Stuff in Person: This was an informal rule that I encountered at several cultures. It goes like this: If you have negative news or feedback to give someone—even as small as a rejected item on an expense report—you are obligated to deliver that news face-to-face. This rule is not easy to follow (it's far more comfortable for both the sender and receiver to communicate electronically), but it works because it deals with tension in an up-front, honest way that avoids misunderstandings and creates shared clarity and connection.

One of the best methods for handling negative news is that of Joe Maddon, the coach of the Chicago Cubs and avowed oenophile. In his office, Maddon keeps a glass bowl filled with slips of paper, each inscribed with the name of an expensive wine. When a player violates a team rule, Maddon asks them to draw a slip of paper out of the bowl, purchase that wine, and uncork it with their manager. In other words, Maddon links the act of discipline to the act of reconnection.

When Forming New Groups, Focus on Two Critical Moments: Jeff Polzer, the Harvard Business School professor who studies organizational behavior (see Chapter 8), traces any group's cooperation norms to two critical moments that happen early in a group's life. They are:

1. The first vulnerability
2. The first disagreement

These small moments are doorways to two possible group paths: *Are we about appearing strong or about exploring the landscape together? Are we about winning interactions, or about learning together?* "At those moments, people either dig in and become defensive and start justifying, and a lot of tension gets created," Polzer says. "Or they say something like, 'Hey, that's interesting. Why don't you agree? I might be wrong, and I'm curious and want to talk about it some more.' What happens in that moment helps set the pattern for everything that follows."

Listen Like a Trampoline: Good listening is about more than nodding attentively; it's about adding insight and creating moments of mutual discovery. Jack Zenger and Joseph Folkman, who run a leadership consultancy, analyzed 3,492 participants in a manager development program and found that the most effective listeners do four things:

1. They interact in ways that make the other person feel safe and supported
2. They take a helping, cooperative stance
3. They occasionally ask questions that gently and constructively challenge old assumptions
4. They make occasional suggestions to open up alternative paths

As Zenger and Folkman put it, the most effective listeners behave like trampolines. They aren't passive sponges. They are active responders, absorbing what the other person gives, supporting them, and adding energy to help the conversation gain velocity and altitude.

Also like trampolines, effective listeners gain amplitude through repetition. When asking questions, they rarely stop at the first response. Rather, they find different ways to explore an area of tension, in order to reveal the truths and connections that will enable cooperation.

"I've found that whenever you ask a question, the first response you get is usually not the answer—it's just the first response," Roshi Givechi says. "So I try to find ways to slowly surface things, to bring out what ought to be shared so that people can build from it. You have to find a lot of ways to ask the same question, and approach the same question from a lot of different angles. Then you have to build questions from that response, to explore more."

In Conversation, Resist the Temptation to Reflexively Add Value: The most important part of creating vulnerability often resides not in what you say but in what you do *not* say. This means having the willpower to forgo easy opportunities to offer solutions and make suggestions. Skilled listeners do not interrupt with phrases like *Hey, here's an idea* or *Let me tell you what worked for me in a similar situation* because they understand that it's not about them. They use a repertoire of gestures and phrases that keep the other person talking. "One of the things I say most often is probably the simplest thing I say," says Givechi. " 'Say more about that.' "

It's not that suggestions are off limits; rather they should be made only after you establish what Givechi calls "a scaffold of thoughtfulness." The scaffold underlies the conversation, supporting the risks and vulnerabilities. With the scaffold, people will be supported in taking the risks that cooperation requires. Without it, the conversation collapses.

Use Candor-Generating Practices like AARs, BrainTrusts, and Red Teaming: While AARs were originally built for the military environment, the tool can be applied to other domains. One good AAR structure is to use five questions:

1. What were our intended results?
2. What were our actual results?
3. What caused our results?
4. What will we do the same next time?
5. What will we do differently?

Some teams also use a Before-Action Review, which is built around a similar set of questions:

1. What are our intended results?
2. What challenges can we anticipate?
3. What have we or others learned from similar situations?
4. What will make us successful this time?

A couple of tips: It may be useful to follow the SEALs' habit of running the AAR without leadership involvement, to boost openness and honesty. Likewise, it may be useful to write down the findings—particularly what will be done the same or differently next time—and share them across the group. After all, the goal of an AAR is not just to figure out what happened but also to build a shared mental model that helps the group navigate future problems.

BrainTrusts, the project-based method pioneered by Pixar, involve assembling a team of experienced leaders who have no formal authority over the project and letting them critique its strengths and weaknesses in a frank and open manner. A key rule of BrainTrusts is that the team is not allowed to suggest solutions, only to highlight problems. This rule maintains the project leaders' ownership of the task, and helps prevent them from assuming a passive, order-taking role.

Red Teaming is a military-derived method for testing strategies; you create a "red team" to come up with ideas to disrupt or defeat your proposed plan. The key is to select a red team that is not wedded to the existing plan in any way, and to give them freedom to think in new ways that the planners might not have anticipated.

AARs, BrainTrusts, and Red Teams each generate the same underlying action: to build the habit of opening up vulnerabilities so that the group can better understand what works, what doesn't work, and how to get better.

Aim for Candor; Avoid Brutal Honesty: Giving honest feedback is tricky, because it can easily result in people feeling hurt or demoralized. One useful distinction, made most clearly at Pixar, is to aim for candor and avoid brutal honesty. By aiming for candor—feedback that is smaller, more targeted, less personal, less judgmental, and equally impactful—it's easier to maintain a sense of safety and belonging in the group.

Embrace the Discomfort: One of the most difficult things about creating habits of vulnerability is that it requires a group to endure two discomforts: emotional pain and a sense of inefficiency. Doing an AAR or a BrainTrust combines the repetition of digging into something that already happened (shouldn't we be moving forward?) with the burning awkwardness inherent in confronting unpleasant truths. But as with any workout, the key is to understand that the pain is not a problem but the path to building a stronger group.

Align Language with Action: Many highly cooperative groups use language to reinforce their interdependence. For example, navy pilots returning to aircraft carriers do not "land" but are "recovered." IDEO doesn't have "project managers"— it has "design community leaders." Groups at Pixar do not offer "notes" on early versions of films; they "plus" them by offering solutions to problems. These might seem like small semantic differences, but they matter because they continually highlight the cooperative, interconnected nature of the work and reinforce the group's shared identity.

Build a Wall Between Performance Review and Professional Development: While it seems natural to hold these two conversations together, in fact it's more effective to keep performance review and professional development separate. Performance evaluation tends to be a high-risk, inevitably judgmental interaction, often with salary-related consequences. Development, on the other hand, is about identifying strengths and providing support and opportunities for growth. Linking them into one conversation muddies the waters. Relatedly, many groups have moved away from ranking workers and shifted to more of a coaching model, where people receive frequent feedback designed to provide them with both a vivid performance snapshot and a path for improvement.

Use Flash Mentoring: One of the best techniques I've seen for creating cooperation in a group is flash mentoring. It is exactly like traditional mentoring—you pick someone you want to learn from and shadow them—except that instead of months or years, it lasts a few hours. Those brief interactions help break down barriers inside a group, build relationships, and facilitate the awareness that fuels helping behavior.

Make the Leader Occasionally Disappear: Several leaders of successful groups have the habit of leaving the group alone at key moments. One of the best at this is Gregg Popovich. Most NBA teams run time-outs according to a choreographed protocol: First the coaches huddle as a group for a few seconds to settle on a message, then they walk over to the bench to deliver that message to the players. However, during about one time-out a month, the Spurs coaches huddle for a time-out . . . and then never walk over to the players. The players sit on the bench, waiting for Popovich to show up. Then, as they belatedly realize he isn't coming, they take charge, start talking among themselves, and figure out a plan.

The New Zealand All-Blacks rugby team have made a habit of this, as players lead several practice sessions each week with little input from the coaches. When I asked Dave Cooper to name the single trait that his best-performing SEAL teams shared, he said, "The best teams tended to be the ones I wasn't that involved with, especially when it came to training. They would disappear and not rely on me at all. They were better at figuring out what they needed to do themselves than I could ever be."

Skill 3

Establish Purpose

13 Three Hundred and
    Eleven Words

One day in 1975 James Burke, president of the health care
company Johnson & Johnson, summoned thirty-five of the
company's senior managers for an unconventional meeting.
They weren't going to talk about strategy or marketing or
planning—or anything to do with business, really. The goal
was to discuss a thirty-two-year-old, one-page document
called the Credo.

The Credo had been written in 1943 by Robert Wood
Johnson, the company's former chairman and a member of
its founding family. Here's how it begins:

> We believe our first responsibility is to doctors,
> nurses, and patients; to mothers and fathers and all
> others who use our products and services. In meeting
> their needs everything we do must be of high quality.
> We must constantly strive to reduce our costs in order
> to maintain reasonable prices. Customers' orders
> must be serviced promptly and accurately.

It goes on like that for four paragraphs, describing the relationship to each group of stakeholders and prioritizing them

as follows: (1) customers, (2) employees, (3) community, and (4) company stockholders. As value statements go, it's a solid one: clear, forthright, and ringing with Old Testament gravitas. (The word *must* appears twenty-one times.) The Credo was prominently displayed at all Johnson & Johnson businesses and was carved into a granite wall at the company's New Jersey headquarters.

The problem, as Burke saw it, was that the Credo didn't seem to matter much to many employees—and what was more, he wasn't sure that it *should* matter. Times had changed. It wasn't that there was an open revolt against the Credo; it was more that Burke picked up a subtle vibe as he traveled around the company and watched people work and interact. As he said later, "A lot of the young people that were coming into Johnson & Johnson really didn't pay much attention to it. Many of them felt that it was kind of a public relations gimmick. It wasn't a unifying document."

Burke's idea was to hold a meeting to determine what role the Credo had in the company's future. When he proposed his idea, many Johnson & Johnson leaders rejected it outright. To question such a foundational document seemed a waste of time. Dick Sellars, chairman of the board, called the notion "ridiculous." He told Burke that challenging the Credo would be like a Catholic deciding to challenge the pope.

Burke, a gravel-voiced Vermonter who'd commanded a landing craft during World War II, didn't back down. "I challenge [the pope] every day when I wake up," he said. "I think at times he's crazy. I think at times my religion is nuts.

Of course I challenge it. Everybody challenges their values, and that's what we ought to do with the Credo." He prevailed.

The meeting was held in a large banquet room. After the managers took their seats, Burke outlined their task. "You guys are in a position of being able to challenge this document, which is the soul of the corporation," he said. "And if you can't live by its principles, we ought to tear it off the walls, because it's an act of pretension to leave it there. And if you want to change it, tell us how it ought to be changed."

With that, the conversation began. "I think [the Credo] should be an absolute," said one manager.

"You can't kid yourself," interrupted another. "The purpose of the business is to make a profit."

Another manager spoke up. "Should we not therefore do what is best for the business, not only what is morally and ethically correct, but what is best for the business by following the Credo so that we do meet [the] needs of society and therefore are able to do things better and decent and human?"

"Charlie, that's motherhood and apple pie, and we're all in agreement with that," said a sharp-voiced man with a comb-over. "The question is, which of these are legitimate demands of society, and how many of these can we fulfill and stay in business."

You get the idea. This wasn't a business meeting; it was closer to a college philosophy seminar. For the entire day, the thirty-six people in that room attempted to locate the company's place in the moral universe; that night some stayed up late putting thoughts to paper. By the end of the process, they reached a consensus to recommit to the existing Credo.

Over the next several years, Burke kept re-creating this conversation, holding Credo challenges at all levels of the company. And the challenges seemed to work; he and others sensed that employees seemed to have a fresh awareness of the Credo. But of course, these kinds of things are mostly intangible, difficult to measure in the course of normal life.

Seven years later, on September 30, 1982, normal life came to an abrupt halt. Burke received a phone call that six people were dead in Chicago because they had ingested his company's product: Extra-Strength Tylenol capsules that had been laced with cyanide. In Chicago, panic ensued. Police roamed the streets using bullhorns to warn people. Boy Scout troops went door to door to alert elderly people who might have missed the warnings. The following day a seventh victim was found, and worries continued to spread. Officials in San Francisco warned residents not to flush their Tylenol down the toilet lest they risk contaminating the sewage system with poison. One news service calculated that the Tylenol poisonings generated the widest U.S. news coverage since the assassination of President Kennedy.

In a few hours, Johnson & Johnson went from being a provider of medicine to being a provider of poison. The atmosphere at headquarters was a mix of shock and disbelief. The larger problem, from Johnson & Johnson's perspective, was that the company was not equipped to deal with this crisis. It didn't have a public affairs division or a system for recalling pills, and its media relations system consisted of a spiral notebook. "It looked like the plague," said David Collins, chairman of McNeil Products, the Johnson subsidiary that made Tylenol. "We had no idea where it would end. And the only information we had was that we didn't know what was going on."

An office at company headquarters was converted into a makeshift war room. Someone located drawing paper and an easel. As information came in—victims, locations, lot numbers of the pills, location of purchase—it was scrawled on sheets of paper, which were then taped to the walls. Before long the walls were draped with urgent questions to which there were no answers. The only certainty was that Tylenol was finished as a business. "I don't think they can ever sell another product under that name," Jerry Della Femina, a legendary advertising guru, told *The New York Times*.

Burke formed a seven-member committee, who started working their way through the cascade of tough decisions. How should they work with law enforcement? What should they tell the public? Most crucially, what should they do with other Tylenol products that were on shelves around the nation?

Four days after the poisonings, Burke and other members of the committee flew to Washington, D.C., to discuss strategy with the FBI and the Food and Drug Administration (FDA). The FBI and the FDA strongly encouraged Burke to limit the recall to Chicago, since no poison had yet been located outside Chicago. A national recall, they said, would needlessly frighten the public, embolden the poisoner, and encourage copycats. And as the FBI didn't need to point out, a larger recall would cost Johnson & Johnson millions of dollars.

Burke and his group thought about it for a while. Then they ignored the advice of the FBI and the FDA and ordered an immediate national recall of every Tylenol product on the market—31 million pills in all—at a cost of $100 million. When Burke was asked for his reasoning behind the decision, the answer came quickly: *We believe our first responsibility is to doctors, nurses, and patients; to mothers and fathers and all others who use our products and services.*

Over the next days and weeks, Johnson & Johnson essentially transformed itself from a pharmaceutical company into a public safety organization. It designed and manufactured innovative tamper-proof packaging; developed exchange, disposal, and refund programs; and built relationships with government, law enforcement, and media. Four weeks after the attacks, it mobilized more than two thousand salespeople to visit doctors and pharmacists to listen to their concerns and inform them of the upcoming changes.

Burke terrified the company's lawyers by making the rounds on the national media, openly expressing his grief and regret and sharing the steps the company was making to ensure the public's safety. Six weeks after the attacks, it introduced new, safer packaging.

And then something unexpected happened. Tylenol's market share, after dropping to zero after the attacks, began a slow climb back to previous levels and continued to grow; one pundit termed it "the greatest comeback since Lazarus."

In ensuing years, Tylenol's response has become the gold standard for handling corporate crisis.

"We had to make hundreds of decisions on the fly; hundreds of people made thousands of decisions," Burke said afterward. "If you look back, we didn't make any bad decisions, really. We really didn't. Those thousands of decisions all had a splendid consistency about them, and that was that the public was going to be served first, because that's who was at stake. So the reason people talk about Tylenol when the Credo discussions come up is that the Credo ran that. Because the hearts and minds of the people who were J&J and who were making the decisions in a whole series of disparate companies . . . they all knew what to do."

On the surface, the story of the Tylenol crisis is about a large group responding to disaster with extraordinary cohesion and focus. But beneath that story lies a curious fact: The key to Johnson & Johnson's extraordinary behavior can be located in a mundane one-page document. The 311 words of the Credo oriented the thinking and behavior of thousands of people as they navigated a complex landscape of choices.

The deeper question is: *How can a handful of simple, forthright sentences make such a difference in a group's behavior?*

In the first two sections of this book we've focused on safety and vulnerability. We've seen how small signals—*You are safe, We share risk here*—connect people and enable them to work together as a single entity. But now it's time to ask: *What's this all for? What are we working toward?*

When I visited the successful groups, I noticed that whenever they communicated anything about their purpose or their values, they were as subtle as a punch in the nose. It started with the surroundings. One expects most groups to fill their surroundings with a few reminders of their mission. These groups, however, did more than that—a lot more.

When you walk into SEAL headquarters at Dam Neck, Virginia, you pass a twisted girder from the World Trade Center bombing, a flag from Mogadishu, and so many memorials to fallen SEALs that it resembles a military museum. Similarly, walking into Pixar's headquarters feels like walking into one of its movies. From the full-size Woody and Buzz made of LEGOs to the twenty-foot-tall Luxo Lamp outside the entrance, everything gleams with Pixarian magic. As for the Upright Citizens Brigade comedy troupe, its basement theater is less a theater than a makeshift hall of fame, its walls plastered with photos of the Harold teams that have made it big. (You can spot a not-yet-famous celebrity in almost every one.) KIPP schools, the highly successful inner-city charter schools, take a similar approach, naming and decorating each classroom to spotlight where the teacher attended college in order to inspire students to do the same, even adorning the bathroom mirrors with an important question: *Where will YOU go to college?*

What's more, the same focus exists within their language. Walking around these places, you tend to hear the same catchphrases and mottoes delivered in the same rhythms.

This is surprising, since you could easily presume that Pixarians would not need to be reminded that *Technology inspires art, and art inspires technology,* that the SEALs would not need to be reminded that it's important to *Shoot, move, and communicate,* and that KIPP students would not need to be reminded to *Work hard and be nice,* given that they say these words many times each day. And yet that is what they do. These groups, who by all rights should know what they stand for, devote a surprising amount of time telling their own story, reminding each other precisely what they stand for—then repeating it ad infinitum. Why?

The first step toward an answer might begin with a small, ordinary-looking songbird called the starling. Like other birds, starlings sometimes congregate in large flocks. When those flocks are threatened by a predator like a falcon, however, they transform into something more. It's called a murmuration, and it's one of the most beautiful and uncanny sights in nature: a living cloud that swirls and changes shape at the speed of thought, forming giant hourglasses, spirals, and tendrils that flow across the sky like a special effect from a Harry Potter movie. A falcon swoops toward a single starling, and at the same instant, on the other side of the flock (thousands of birds away), the other birds instantly sense it and react as one to flow away from the danger. The question, of course, is how so many birds behave like a single entity. Early naturalists theorized that starlings possessed some quasi-mystical ESP to perceive and plan group movements. One British scientist termed it "telepathy"; another called it "biological radio."

The real reason, demonstrated in a 2007 study by a team of theoretical physicists from the University of Rome, is that the starlings' cohesion is built on relentless attention to a small set of signals. Basically, each starling tracks the six or seven birds closest to it, sending and receiving cues of direction, speed, acceleration, and distance. That shared habit of intensive, up-close watching, amplified through the flock, allows the group to behave as one. In other words, the reason starling flocks can behave so intelligently has nothing to do with telepathy or magic and everything to do with a simpler ability: to pay focused attention to a small handful of key markers.

This idea helps give us a window into how successful cultures create and sustain purpose. Successful groups are attuned to the same truth as the starlings: Purpose isn't about tapping into some mystical internal drive but rather about creating simple beacons that focus attention and engagement on the shared goal. Successful cultures do this by relentlessly seeking ways to tell and retell their story. To do this, they build what we'll call high-purpose environments.

High-purpose environments are filled with small, vivid signals designed to create a link between the present moment and a future ideal. They provide the two simple locators that every navigation process requires: *Here is where we are* and *Here is where we want to go*. The surprising thing, from a scientific point of view, is how responsive we are to this pattern of signaling.

A few years ago a professor of psychology named Gabriele Oettingen set out to perform what might rank as the most basic psychological experiment of all time. In fact, you can do it right now. It goes like this:

Step 1: Think about a realistic goal that you'd like to achieve. It could be anything: Become skilled at a sport, re-dedicate yourself to a relationship, lose a few pounds, get a new job. Spend a few seconds reflecting on that goal and imagining that it's come true. Picture a future where you've achieved it.

Got it?

Step 2: Take a few seconds and picture the obstacles be-tween you and that goal as vividly as possible. Don't gloss over the negatives, but try to see them as they truly are. For example, if you were trying to lose weight, you might pic-ture those moments of weakness when you smell warm cookies, and you decide to eat one (or three).

That's it. It's called mental contrasting, and it seems less like science than the kind of advice you might come across on a late-night infomercial: *Envision a reachable goal, and envision the obstacles*. The thing is, as Oettingen discovered, this method works, triggering significant changes in behav-ior and motivation. In one study, adolescents preparing for the PSAT who used this method chose to complete 60 per-cent more practice questions than the control group. In an-other, dieters consumed significantly fewer calories, were more physically active, and lost more weight.

Mental contrasting has also been shown to improve the ability to interact positively with strangers, negotiate deals, speak in public, manage time, improve communication, and perform a range of other skills. As Oettingen wrote, "The conjoint elaboration of the future and the present reality

makes both simultaneously accessible and links them together in the sense that the reality stands in the way of realizing the desired future."

Oettingen's work doesn't line up with how we normally
think about motivation and goals. We normally think about
them as being intrinsic to a person. People are either motivated or they're not; accordingly, we describe motivation
with terms like *desire* or *heart*. But in these experiments,
motivation is not a possession but rather the result of a two-
part process of channeling your attention: *Here's where
you're at* and *Here's where you want to go*.

That shared future could be a goal or a behavior. (*We put
customer safety first. We shoot, move, and communicate*.) It
doesn't matter. What matters is establishing this link and
consistently creating engagement around it. What matters is
telling the story.

We tend to use the word *story* casually, as if stories and
narratives were ephemeral decorations for some unchanging
underlying reality. The deeper neurological truth is that stories do not cloak reality but create it, triggering cascades of
perception and motivation. The proof is in brain scans:
When we hear a fact, a few isolated areas of our brain light
up, translating words and meanings. When we hear a story,
however, our brain lights up like Las Vegas, tracing the
chains of cause, effect, and meaning. Stories are not just stories; they are the best invention ever created for delivering
mental models that drive behavior.

Think for a moment about the jungle of decisions Johnson & Johnson leaders faced in the days after the Tylenol
poisonings. It is not easy to spend $100 million against the

advice of federal officials (or to explain that decision to stockholders and a board of trustees). It is not easy to repurpose thousands of people into new and unfamiliar roles (or to explain why they should embrace that change). One would presume that these decisions and actions would have felt painful or agonizing.

And yet Burke doesn't describe them as painful or agonizing. He describes them as straightforward. "Well, I got a lot of credit for that," he told a reporter. "But the fact is my job was made not only simple, but . . . there wasn't anything else I could have done. Every person who worked for Johnson & Johnson in the world was watching the poisonings. . . . If we had done anything other than what we did, think about how those employees would have felt. I mean, the very soul of the corporation was watching us."

In other words, Burke and his team felt a bit like starlings in a flock feel. They moved as one because they were attuned to the same clear signal of the Credo resonating through the group. *We believe our first responsibility is to doctors, nurses, and patients; to mothers and fathers and all others who use our products and services.* The difficult choices they made weren't really all that difficult. They were closer to a reflex.

The main challenge to understanding how stories guide group behavior is that stories are hard to isolate. Stories are like air: everywhere and nowhere at the same time. How do you measure the effect of a narrative?

Fortunately for us, back in 1965, a Harvard psychologist

named Robert Rosenthal found a way. He approached a California public elementary school and offered to test the school's students with a newly developed intelligence-identification tool, called the Harvard Test of Inflected Acquisition, which could accurately predict which children would excel academically in the coming year. The school naturally agreed, and the test was administered to the entire student body. A few weeks later, teachers were provided with the names of the children (about 20 percent of the student body) who had tested as high-potentials. These particular children, the teachers were informed, were special. Though they might not have performed well in the past, the test indicated that they possessed "unusual potential for intellectual growth." (The students were not informed of the test results.)

The following year Rosenthal returned to measure how the high-potential students had performed. Exactly as the test had predicted, the first- and second-grade high-potentials had succeeded to a remarkable degree: The first-graders gained 27 IQ points (versus 12 points for the rest of the class); and the second-graders gained 17 points (versus 7 points). In addition, the high-potentials thrived in ways that went beyond measurement. They were described by their teachers as being more curious, happier, better adjusted, and more likely to experience success as adults. What's more, the teachers reported that they had enjoyed teaching that year more than any year in the past.

Here's the twist: the Harvard Test of Inflected Acquisition was complete baloney. In fact, the "high-potentials" had been selected at random. The real subject of the test was not the students but the narratives that drive the relationship between the teachers and the students.

What happened, Rosenthal discovered, was replacing one story—*These are average kids*—with a new one—*These are special kids, destined to succeed*—served as a locator beacon that reoriented the teachers, creating a cascade of behaviors that guided the student toward that future. It didn't matter that the story was false, or that the children were, in fact, randomly selected. The simple, glowing idea—*This child has unusual potential for intellectual growth*—aligned motivations, awareness, and behaviors. Rosenthal classified the changes into four categories.

1. Warmth (the teachers were kinder, more attentive, and more connective)
2. Input (the teachers provided more material for learning)
3. Response-opportunity (the teachers called on the students more often, and listened more carefully)
4. Feedback (the teachers provided more, especially when the student made a mistake)

The interesting thing about these changes is how small they are, consisting of thousands of tiny behaviors over the school year. Every time the teacher interacted with the student, a connection lit up in the teacher's brain between the present and the future. Each time the student did something ambiguous, the teacher gave the student the benefit of the doubt. Each time the student made a mistake, the teacher presumed that the student needed better feedback. By themselves, each of these behaviors meant little. Together, they created a virtuous spiral that helped students thrive in ways that exceeded their so-called limits.

This virtuous spiral can be sparked by other methods as well. A good example was used in an experiment by Adam Grant, an author and organizational psychologist at the Wharton School of the University of Pennsylvania, whose work we encountered in Chapter 6. A few years back Grant was asked by the University of Michigan to look into the low performance of its call center workers who phoned university alumni and asked them to donate money. The work was repetitive and tedious, and the rejection rate stood at a solid 93 percent. The university had tried several incentives to improve performance, such as prizes and contests, to no avail.

Grant knew that some of the money raised at the call center went toward scholarships. He wondered if the workers would be more motivated if they knew more about the real-world uses of that money. So he tracked down one of the scholarship recipients, a student named Will, and asked him to write a letter about what his scholarship meant to him. Here is an excerpt:

> When it came down to making the decision, I discovered that the out-of-state tuition was quite expensive. But this university is in my blood. My grandparents met here. My dad and his four brothers all went here. I even owe my younger brother to this school—he was conceived the night we won the NCAA basketball tournament. All my life I have

dreamed of coming here. I was ecstatic to receive the scholarship, and I came to school ready to take full advantage of the opportunities it afforded me. The scholarship has improved my life in many ways.

After Grant shared Will's letter with the call center workers, he saw an immediate boost in calls and donations. So he took the next step. Rather than merely read call center workers a letter, Grant brought in scholarship recipients for in-person visits. The visits lasted five minutes. They weren't complex; each student shared their story as Will had done: *Here's where I came from. Here's what the money raised by your work means to me.* Over the next month, time spent calling increased 142 percent, and weekly revenues increased 172 percent. The incentives hadn't changed. The task hadn't changed. All that had changed was the fact that the workers had received a clear beacon of purpose, and it made all the difference.

What happened in Rosenthal's and Grant's experiments is no different from what happened when Johnson & Johnson gathered to challenge the Credo. They created a high-purpose environment, flooded the zone with signals that linked the present effort to a meaningful future, and used a single story to orient motivation the way that a magnetic field orients a compass needle to true north: *This is why we work. Here is where you should put your energy.*

In the next chapter, we'll focus on real-world ways in which high-purpose environments are established and nurtured. And a good way to begin is to examine two cases where those environments were built against the odds. The first involves an innovative attempt to control some of the most dangerous soccer hooligans on the planet. The second involves teams of doctors learning to perform a revolutionary surgical innovation.

14

The Hooligans and
the Surgeons

Taming the Hooligans

Portugal was about to get wrecked.

It was the eve of the 2004 European Championships, an every-four-years soccer tournament that ranks second only to the World Cup in size and spectacle. Hundreds of thousands of fans were streaming toward sparkling venues across this sunny nation. For Portugal, this was a big moment, its coming-out party on the world sporting stage. There was just one problem, and it was the same problem that has shadowed European soccer for decades: English soccer hooligans.

The Portuguese organizers knew what they were up against because the previous championships, held four years earlier in Belgium, had provided a vivid lesson. The Belgian police had prepared well for the hooligans, spending millions training their force and equipping themselves with the best antiriot equipment, surveillance cameras, and information systems available. They had worked closely with the British government to identify and bar known troublemakers from entering the country. In short, they had been as ready as it was possible to be. And none of it had helped.

Thousands of English hooligans, showing the sort of unified resolve their team has historically lacked, roamed wild, smashing shop windows, beating up bystanders, and battling riot police wielding batons, fire hoses, and tear gas. By tournament's end, more than one thousand English supporters were arrested, tournament organizers considered banishing the English team from the tournament, and pundits were wondering whether international tournaments might be a thing of the past.

According to most social scientists, this reality was both logical and historically unavoidable, as English hooligans embodied the working-class aggression known as the English Disease. Decades of experience showed that the disease could not be cured, only its symptoms controlled. As the 2004 tournament approached, riots seemed inevitable. As one English writer put it, sunny Portugal was about to become the target of the "biggest English invasion since D-Day." To prepare, the Portuguese government purchased $21 million of riot-control tools: water cannons, truncheons, pepper spray, and police dogs. It also looked at new approaches, including the work of an obscure Liverpool University social psychologist named Clifford Stott.

Stott is a plainspoken, crew-cut man who specializes in crowd violence. He studied the Los Angeles riots of 1992 and the U.K. poll tax riots of 1990, and as the 2004 championships approached, he was working on a new theory that had less to do with the forces of social history than with social cues. His idea was that it was possible to stop crowd violence by changing the signals the police were transmitting. In his view, riot gear and armored cars were cues that activated hooligan behavior in fans who might otherwise behave normally. (Ninety-five percent of the people arrested for soccer violence, his research showed, had no prior history of disorderly conduct.) Stott believed that the key to policing riots was to essentially stop policing riots.

Stott's early trials of his model were sufficiently compelling, and the Portuguese authorities were sufficiently desperate, that Stott found himself, to his everlasting surprise, in charge of a high-stakes experiment: Could the most dangerous soccer hooligans in the world be stopped by a handful of social cues?

First, Stott set about training the Portuguese police. Rule number one was to keep all riot gear out of sight: no phalanxes of helmeted cops, no armored vehicles, no riot shields and batons. Instead, Stott trained a crew of liaison officers who wore light-blue vests instead of the customary yellow. These officers were selected not for their riot control skills but for their social skills: friendliness and ability to banter. Stott encouraged them to study up on the teams and fans and get good at making small talk about the coaches, on-field strategies, and team gossip. "We sought out people who had the gift of the gab," he says, "who could throw their arm around someone and chat with them about anything."

The bigger challenge for Stott was rewiring police instincts. The English hooligans had a habit of kicking soccer balls in public places, booting the ball high into the air and down onto the heads and café tables of bystanders, thus igniting the kind of small-scale confrontations of which riots are born. Conventional police procedure is to immediately and forcibly intervene and confiscate the ball before any open fighting breaks out. But on Stott's advice, Portuguese officers were instructed to do something more difficult: to wait until the hooligans kicked the ball within reach of the police. Then and only then could the police take the ball and keep it.

"You have to play by the shared rules," Stott says. "The police can't just go take the ball, because that's precisely the kind of disproportionate use of force that creates the problem. If you wait until the ball comes to you and simply hang on to it, the crowd sees it as legitimate."

To some Portuguese police, Stott's ideas sounded illogical if not insane. Several protested, saying that facing gangs of violent hooligans without protective armor was reckless. By the time the tournament arrived, the English press had derisively termed the program "Hug-A-Thug." The sporting and scientific worlds waited doubtfully to see if Stott's method would work.

It worked. More than one million fans visited the country over the three-week-long tournament, and in areas that used Stott's approach, only one English fan was arrested. Observers recorded two thousand crowd-police interactions, of which only 0.4 percent qualified as disorderly. The only incidents of violence occurred in an area that was policed according to the old-fashioned helmet-and-shield system.

In the ensuing years, Stott's approach has become the model for controlling sport-related violence in Europe and around the globe. One of the reasons it works is that it creates a high-purpose environment by delivering an unbroken array of consistent little signals. Every time an officer banters with a fan, every time a fan notices the lack of protective armor, a signal is sent: *We are here to get along*. Every time the police allow fans to keep kicking the ball, they reinforce that signal. By themselves, none of the signals matter. Together they build a new story.

For Stott, the most revealing moment in Portugal came halfway through the tournament when a yellow-vested Portuguese policeman had an encounter with an overly exuberant English fan. The policeman tried to calm the fan; the fan resisted, and then the policeman reflexively used force, grabbing the fan roughly. A ripple of energy moved through the crowd; people shouted and pushed. It was exactly the kind of situation Stott feared most: a single overuse of force that could cause a disastrous spiral.

But that didn't happen. Instead, the fans shouted out to one of the blue-vested liaison officers. "The fans called over to the liaison and said, 'Hey, can you come and sort this policeman out for us?'" Stott says. "The roles had reversed, and the fans were policing the police. They had socially bonded with the liaisons. They saw them as their advocate."

The Fastest Learners

One of the best measures of any group's culture is its learning velocity—how quickly it improves its performance of a new skill. In 1998, a team of Harvard researchers led by Amy Edmondson (whom we met in Chapter 1) tracked the learning velocity of sixteen surgical teams learning to perform a new heart surgery technique. The technique was called MICS, minimally invasive cardiac surgery, and it involved performing coronary artery bypass grafts and valve repairs through a small chest incision rather than by sawing the breastbone in half. Each of the sixteen teams took the identical three-day training program, then returned to their hospitals and started performing the procedure. The question was, which team would learn the fastest and most effectively?

At the outset, the Chelsea Hospital team looked like it would win.* Chelsea was an elite teaching hospital in a metropolitan area. Its cardiac surgery team was led by Dr. C, a nationally recognized expert who had been involved designing the MICS technology and who had already performed more than sixty procedures using the method. In addition, Chelsea had a strong organizational commitment to the new procedure, which it demonstrated by sending several department heads to the training course.

At the other end of the scale was the team from Mountain Medical Center, which was smaller, not a teaching institution, and located in a rural area. Its team was led by Dr. M, a young surgeon who had never done the MICS procedure and who had a similarly inexperienced team around him.

If you had to predict which team would perform better, Chelsea would be the logical choice. It had more expertise, more experience, and more organizational support than Mountain Medical. But as it turned out, Chelsea's team did not win. To the contrary: It was slower to learn, and its skill (measured by the time it took to successfully complete the MICS surgery) plateaued after ten procedures. What's more,

---

* The names of the hospitals and doctors were altered in the study.

the team members weren't happy: In interviews afterward, they reported feeling dissatisfied. After six months, Chelsea ranked tenth out of sixteen teams.

The Mountain Medical team, on the other hand, learned fast and well. By the fifth surgery, its members were already faster than Chelsea's top mark. By the twentieth procedure, Mountain Medical was completing successful surgeries a full hour faster than Chelsea and, more important, was reporting high rates of efficiency and satisfaction. After six months, Mountain Medical ranked second out of the sixteen teams.

This feast-or-famine pattern wasn't unique to these two hospitals. When Edmondson plotted the results, she found that hospitals fell into two groups: teams that had high success and teams that had low success. It wasn't a bell curve; it was more like a split screen. Teams were either like Mountain Medical or like Chelsea; they either clicked or they didn't. Why?

The answer, Edmondson discovered, lay in the patterns of real-time signals through which the team members were connected (or not) with the purpose of the work. These signals consisted of five basic types:

1. *Framing*: Successful teams conceptualized MICS as a learning experience that would benefit patients and the hospital. Unsuccessful teams conceptualized MICS as an add-on to existing practices.
2. *Roles*: Successful teams were explicitly told by the team leader why their individual and collective skills were important for the team's success, and

why it was important for them to perform as a team. Unsuccessful teams were not.

3. *Rehearsal*: Successful teams did elaborate dry runs of the procedure, preparing in detail, explaining the new protocols, and talking about communication. Unsuccessful teams took minimal steps to prepare.

4. *Explicit encouragement to speak up*: Successful teams were told by team leaders to speak up if they saw a problem; they were actively coached through the feedback process. The leaders of unsuccessful teams did little coaching, and as a result team members were hesitant to speak up.

5. *Active reflection:* Between surgeries, successful teams went over performance, discussed future cases, and suggested improvements. For example, the team leader at Mountain Medical wore a head-mounted camera during surgery to help facilitate discussion and feedback. Unsuccessful teams tended not to do this.

Note what factors are *not* on this list: experience, surgeon status, and organizational support. These qualities mattered far less than the simple, steady pulse of real-time signals that channeled attention toward the larger goal. Sometimes those signals involved the hospital (*MICS is an important learning opportunity*); sometimes the patient (*Patients will benefit*); sometimes the team member (*You have a role and a future with this team*); sometimes they placed value on rehearsal or reflection. But they all performed the same vital function: to flood the environment with narrative links between what they were doing now and what it meant.

The other feature of this list is that many of these signals could easily be viewed as obvious and redundant. For instance, do highly experienced professionals like nurses and anesthesiologists really need to be explicitly told that their role *in a cardiac surgery* is important? Do they really need to be informed that if they see the surgeon make a mistake, they might want to speak up?

The answer, as Edmondson discovered, is a thundering yes. The value of those signals is not in their information but in the fact that they orient the team to the task and to one another. What seems like repetition is, in fact, navigation. Those signals added up in a way that you can hear in team members' voices. Listen to these quotes from the successful teams:

[Surgeon] "The ability of the surgeon to allow himself to become a partner, not a dictator, is critical. For example, you really do have to change what you're doing [during an operation] based on a suggestion from someone else on the team."

[Nurse] "We all have to share the knowledge. For example, in the last case, we needed to insert a guidewire, and I grabbed the wrong wire and I didn't recognize it at first. And my circulating nurse said, 'Sue, you grabbed the wrong wire.' This shows how much the different roles don't matter. We all have to know about everything. You have to work as a team."

[Nurse] "Every time we are going to do a [MICS] procedure I feel like I've been enlightened. I can see these patients doing so well. . . . It is such a rewarding experience. I am so grateful I was picked."

Now listen to these quotes from the unsuccessful teams:

[Surgeon] "Once I get a team set up, I never look up [from the operating field]. It's they who have to make sure everything is flowing."

[Anesthesiologist] "I wouldn't speak up if I weren't confident that a mistake would lead to an adverse outcome. I'm not comfortable hypothesizing."

[Nurse] "If I see a MICS case on the list [for tomorrow] I think 'Oh! Do we really have to do it? Just get me a fresh blade so I can slash my wrists right now.'"

These voices sound like they are coming from different universes. Ironically, both were doing the exact same procedure with the exact same training. The only difference was that one group received clear beacons of meaning throughout the process, and the other didn't. The difference wasn't in who they were but in the set of small, attentive, consistent links between where they are now and where they are headed.

This is the way high-purpose environments work. They are about sending not so much one big signal as a handful of steady, ultra-clear signals that are aligned with a shared goal. They are less about being inspiring than about being consistent. They are found not within big speeches so much as within everyday moments when people can sense the message: *This is why we work; this is what we are aiming for.*

Now that we've established the basic mechanism of high-purpose environments, let's explore the next question: *How do you create one?* The answer, it turns out, depends on the type of skills you want your group to perform. *High-proficiency environments* help a group deliver a well-defined, reliable performance, while *high-creativity environments* help a group create something new. This distinction is important because it highlights the two basic challenges facing any group: consistency and innovation. And as we're about to see, building purpose in these two areas requires different approaches.

15 How to Lead for Proficiency

When you think of the planet's most challenging environments, you tend to envision places like Death Valley or Antarctica: unforgiving landscapes that relentlessly expose weakness. You don't tend to think of the New York restaurant scene. That is, until you consider the survival rates.

Each year around a thousand new restaurants open in New York City. All are launched with optimism, confidence, and high hopes for success. Five years later eight hundred of them have vanished without a trace, for various reasons that are, in essence, the same reason. A successful restaurant, like a successful Antarctic expedition, depends on ceaseless proficiency. Good food is not enough. Good location is not enough. Good service, training, branding, leadership, adaptability, and luck are not enough. Survival depends on putting all of it together, night after night. If you fail, you disappear.

Within this unforgiving ecosystem, Danny Meyer has built a record that is not as unlikely as it is inconceivable. Over the past thirty years, he has opened twenty-five restaurants. Except for one, they are all successful—and not just a little bit. Union Square Cafe, Meyer's first restaurant, has won the top spot in *Zagat*'s best-restaurant rankings an unprecedented nine times; his other restaurants routinely occupy as much as a quarter of the top twenty, and his restaurants and chefs have won twenty-six James Beard awards. Perhaps more impressively, each of Meyer's restaurants is unique, varying from a tavern to a barbecue joint, to an Italian café, to a fast-casual burger chain called Shake Shack that is now worth $1.5 billion.

The reason Meyer's restaurants are successful is the warm, connective feeling they create, a feeling that can be summed up in one word: *home*. When you walk into a Meyer restaurant, you feel that you are being cared for. This feeling radiates from the surroundings and the food but most of all from the people, who approach each interaction with familial thoughtfulness. When I asked Meyer's guests and employees for examples of moments where this feeling was created, they offered the following two stories.

A young woman, recently moved to New York from the Midwest, took her parents out to dinner at 11 Madison Park to celebrate her new start in the big city—and to allay her parents' fears about the difficulties of living in New York. Toward the end of dinner, as they looked over the dessert menu, the father pointed to a forty-two-dollar glass of dessert wine called Château d'Yquem and commented on how insanely expensive New York was. The waiter overheard the father's comment and, moments later, reappeared carrying a bottle of Château d'Yquem and three glasses. The waiter said, "We are so grateful you came tonight. I heard you talking about the Château d'Yquem. This is one of the rarest and best dessert wines in the entire world, and we would love to offer you each a taste with our compliments." A small explosion of surprise and delight ensued.

Then there was the time a dining companion of Nebraska senator Bob Kerrey found a beetle in his salad at Gramercy Tavern. The next day Kerrey and his friends were eating at another of Meyer's restaurants. After they were seated, a salad arrived garnished with a small piece of paper on which the word *Ringo* was written. The waiter said, "Danny wanted to make sure you knew that Gramercy Tavern wasn't the only one of his restaurants that's willing to garnish your salad with a Beatle."

If you mention that it's your anniversary or your birthday, the restaurant will remember. If you prefer a table by the window, it will remember. If you prefer the crusty ends of bread, it will remember.* These tasks are not simple, because they depend on an unbroken chain of awareness and action. The waiter who brought the Château d'Yquem had to (1) be alert to the dynamic between the excited, hopeful young woman and her worried parents; (2) notice the father's comment about the wine; (3) connect it to an idea; (4) be empowered to spend the restaurant's money on a gesture; and (5) deliver that gesture with grace. At any point, the chain could have been broken, and no one would have noticed. But the chain wasn't broken, and so it created the signature upwelling of warm emotion that has carried Mey-

---

* Much of this remembering takes place within the reservations system, where guest preferences are religiously noted by waitstaff and managers. I saw one guest note that read: *Likes extra butter with bread; needs a lot of love.*

er's ventures to success. The question is, how does Meyer accomplish this so reliably at so many restaurants?

When you sit down across the table from Danny Meyer, his eyes lock on you in a mix of interest and empathy. His body language is relaxed and alert but unhurried. His voice is steady, with a midwestern earnestness that's vaguely reminiscent of Jimmy Stewart. If you ask him a question—say, what's the best hamburger in New York—he pauses before answering. He has devoted hundreds of hours to exploring this question, so he knows a great deal. But when he answers, that answer has nothing to do with his knowledge and everything to do with you.

"Well," he says. "What kind of hamburger you like depends on what kind of mood you're in."

We're in Maialino, one of his restaurants near Gramercy Park, and it's breakfast. Around us the Meyerian universe is spinning contentedly: fresh flowers burst from ceramic vases, and happy diners chat with attentive waiters. We're talking about how Meyer studied political science at Trinity College and how he worked for a presidential campaign (which helped him see every worker as basically a volunteer) when, behind me, a tray accidentally slips from a waiter's hand, and several water glasses smash on the floor.

For a microsecond, all the action stops. Meyer raises a finger, pressing pause on our conversation so he can watch what happens. The waiter who dropped the glasses starts picking up the pieces, and another waiter arrives with a broom and a dustpan. The cleanup happens swiftly, and everyone turns back to their food. Then I ask Meyer why he was watching so closely.

"I'm watching for what happens right afterward, and I'm looking for their energy level to go up," he says. "They connect to clean up the problem, and the energy level goes either up or down, and if we're doing our job right, their energy level will go up." He puts his fists together, and then makes an explosion gesture with his fingers. "They are creating uplifting energy that has nothing to do with the task and everything to do with each other and what comes next. It's not really that different from an ant colony or a beehive. Every action adds on to the others."

I ask Meyer what a bad interaction looks like. "It's one of two things," he says. "Either they're disinterested—'I'm just doing my job' kind of thing. Or they're angry at the other person or the situation. And if I were to see that, I would know that there's a deeper problem here, because the number-one job is to take care of each other. I didn't always know that, but I know it now."

Meyer starts telling me about his background: his youth in St. Louis, the early fascination with food and travel, the emotionally distant father who was in the hotel and food business, Meyer's last-second veer away from law school and into the restaurant business, and finally the mid-1980s and the early days of Union Square Cafe, where his education really began.

"I didn't know how to read a balance sheet," he says. "I didn't know how to manage flow or run a kitchen. I didn't know anything. But I did know how I wanted to make people feel. I wanted them to feel like they couldn't tell if they had stayed home or gone out."

To do that, Meyer relied on instinct. He hired midwesterners to increase friendliness. He trained the staff himself, playacting various waiter-diner scenarios. When service was slow, as it often was in the early days, he placated guests with free wine and gave the staff latitude to provide treats. He made a habit of gathering tidbits of information to help his guests feel more at home. He paid particular attention to language. He hated waiter-speak like "Are you still working on that?" (it's not work!) or "Is everything to your liking?" (so impersonal!). Instead, he sought to create language that gave guests the feeling that the staff was on their side. For instance, when a reservation was unavailable, he would say, "Can you give me a range of times that work for you, so I can root for a cancellation?"

Union Square Cafe was a huge success, with the ever-present Meyer working the door, busing tables, and cleaning up spills. Then in 1995 he opened a second restaurant, Gramercy Tavern. And that's when things got difficult. Service started to slip. Food was inconsistent. Customers were unhappy. Meyer would split his time between the two restaurants trying frantically to boost performance, but it wasn't working. "It was a complete nightmare," he says. "I was miserable. I was running back and forth between the two places, and neither of them was doing as well as I wanted. It was kind of a classic situation. I mean, this is why most people who open a restaurant open only one."

It all came to a head one day that fall at Gramercy Tavern, when a regular customer who was hosting a lunch for six ordered salmon. She ate about half of it, then told the waiter that she didn't care for it—could she have something else? The waiter brought a new dish, then asked Gramercy's manager whether the salmon should stay on the woman's bill. The manager said it should. After all, the woman had eaten more than half of the dish, and there had been nothing wrong with the salmon. When the woman paid, she was handed a doggie bag with the remains of her salmon. When the woman got home, she wrote to Meyer, "I can't believe how insulting and passive-aggressive this was, and it's not what I would expect at one of your restaurants."

"She was absolutely right," Meyer says. "And here's the worst part: Everybody at Gramercy thought they were doing a good job. The manager thought they were doing a good job. The waiter thought they were doing a good job. Everybody stood there and watched this happen, and nobody stopped it. We had spent hours and hours training people not to do this kind of thing, but they were doing it, and we had no control. That's when I knew that I had to find a way to build a language, to teach behavior. I could no longer just model the behavior and trust that people would understand and do it. I had to start naming stuff."

A few weeks later Meyer invited the entire staff to a Saturday retreat along the Hudson River and started a conversation about values: *What were they really about? What did they stand for? Who came first?*

"That salmon incident was the Plymouth Rock moment," says Richard Coraine, chief development officer of the Union Square Hospitality Group, the parent company for Meyer's restaurants. "Danny realized that he needed to be in two places at once. Which meant that he had to find a way to deliver the signal. People will respond to what their boss feels is important. So Danny had to define and articulate what was important."

At the retreat, Meyer and the staff ranked their priorities:

1. Colleagues
2. Guests
3. Community
4. Suppliers
5. Investors

For Meyer, this was a breakthrough. "Naming these things felt incredibly good," he says. "Getting all this out in the open. The manager who'd caused the salmon problem ended up leaving, and that's when things started to take off, and I realized that how we treat each other is everything. If we do that well, everything else will fall into place."

In a similar way, Meyer then attempted to name the specific behaviors and interactions he wanted to create at his restaurants. He already had an assortment of catchphrases that he used informally in training—he had a knack for distilling ideas into handy maxims. But now he started paying deeper attention to these phrases, thinking about them as tools. Here are a few:

Read the guest
Athletic hospitality
Writing a great final chapter
Turning up the Home Dial

Loving problems

Finding the yes

Collecting the dots and connecting the dots

Creating raves for guests

One size fits one

Skunking

Making the charitable assumption

Planting like seeds in like gardens

Put us out of business with your generosity

Be aware of your emotional wake

To get a hug, you have to give a hug

The excellence reflex

Are you an agent or a gatekeeper?

On the surface, these look like garden-variety corporate aphorisms. In fact, each of them functions as a small narrative in itself, providing a vivid mental model for solving the routine problems the staff faced. *Making the charitable assumption* means that when someone behaves poorly, you should avoid judging them and instead give them the benefit of the doubt. *Collecting the dots* means gathering information about guests; *connecting the dots* is using that information to create happiness. *Skunking* is spraying negative energy into the workplace, as skunks do when they're frightened. By themselves, these phrases are unremarkable. But together, endlessly repeated and modeled through behavior, they create a larger conceptual framework that connects with the group's identity and expresses its core purpose: *We take care of people.*

Meyer became more intentional about embedding his

catchphrases and stating priorities in training, staff meetings, and all communications. He pushed his leaders to seek opportunities to use and model the key behaviors. He began to treat his role as that of a culture broadcaster. And it worked. In a few months, the atmosphere at both restaurants improved markedly. Meyer kept it up, steadily expanding and refining the language. "You have priorities, whether you name them or not," he says. "If you want to grow, you'd better name them, and you'd better name the behaviors that support the priorities."

A couple years after the salmon incident, an NYU doctoral student in organizational behavior named Susan Reilly Salgado became curious about why Meyer's restaurants felt so different from all others. As she chatted with the waitstaff, she noticed that they all tended to describe their jobs with the same words: *home, family, warmth*. She approached Meyer and asked him if she could make the restaurant the subject of her research, and he agreed, provided she took a job there. Salgado worked at Union Square Cafe for six months. She watched the way the staff members interacted with one another and with customers, and she noticed what she called "micro-processes" that drove those interactions. Here is how she summed up her findings in her dissertation: "The results indicate that Union Square Cafe achieves its differentiation strategy of 'enlightened hospitality' through a synergistic set of human resource management practices involving three key practices: selection of employees based on emotional capabilities, respectful treatment of employees, and management through a simple set of rules that stimulate complex and intricate behaviors benefiting customers."

A simple set of rules that stimulate complex and intricate behaviors benefiting customers. Salgado discovered, in other words, that Meyer succeeded for the same reason James Burke succeeded with the Credo challenge. Creating engagement around a clear, simple set of priorities can function as a lighthouse, orienting behavior and providing a path toward a goal.

All of which raises the deeper question of how exactly this happens, how a handful of catchphrases and a list of priorities can produce such smooth and proficient performance. We can get an answer from an unlikely source: a tiny organism called a slime mold.

Slime molds are ancient, bloblike organisms made up of thousands of individual amoebae. Most of the time slime molds are passive, sedate, and wholly unremarkable. But when food becomes scarce, the thousands of amoebae begin to work together in a beautiful and intelligent way. Back in the 1940s, a Harvard undergraduate named John Tyler Bonner photographed slime molds with a time-lapse camera and made a film, which he began to show to academic audiences. Word spread, and before long lecture halls were overflowing with enraptured crowds. Albert Einstein requested a private viewing. J. J. O'Neill of the *New York Herald Tribune* told Bonner that his work was more important than the discovery of the atomic bomb.

The film's first frames show a disconnected scattering of small gray blobs. But then, as if responding to an invisible signal, the amoebae move with single intent toward the center, where thousands of them fuse together into a single organism that starts to move. At the tip of the organism, another transformation happens as some of the amoebae crawl upward, forming a stalk. Other amoebae crawl over them, where they become spores, to blow off in the wind and reproduce. The whole thing is utterly magical and orchestral, as if some hidden conductor were whispering instructions: *You over here, now here, now all together*. The film became a sensation because it embodied a profound mystery: How does this kind of intelligent group behavior happen with creatures that possess no intelligence?

For years, researchers presumed that the behavior was a result of an "organizer cell" that functioned as a kind of biological drill sergeant, telling the others what to do and when. This organizer cell, it turns out, does not exist. What does exist is something more powerful: a simple set of rules called heuristics that drive behavior.

"We assume that because we're complex, that the way we make decisions is also complex," says Madeleine Beekman, who studies slime molds at the University of Sydney. "But in reality, we're using very simple rules of thumb. The slime mold shows us that it's possible for groups to solve extremely complex problems using a few rules of thumb."

In the case of slime molds, these rules of thumb are as follows:

If there's no food, connect with one another.
If connected, stay connected and move toward the
   light.
If you reach the light, stay connected and climb.

"Honeybees work the same way," Beekman says. "So do ants and many other species. They all use decision-making heuristics. There's no reason we wouldn't use it too. If you look at these species, you can feel the connection. Like us, they all seek a collective goal."

Beekman and the slime molds give us a new way to think about why Danny Meyer's catchphrases work so well. They are not merely catchphrases; they are heuristics that provide guidance by creating if/then scenarios in a vivid, memorable way. Structurally, there is no difference between *If someone is rude, make a charitable assumption* and *If there's no food, connect with one another*. Both function as a conceptual beacon, creating situational awareness and providing clarity in times of potential confusion. This is why so many of Meyer's catchphrases focus on how to respond to mistakes.

> You can't prevent mistakes, but you can solve problems graciously.
> If it ain't broke, fix it.
> Mistakes are like waves; servers are really surfers.
> The road to success is paved with mistakes well handled.

The trick is not just to send the signal but to create engagement around it. This is where Meyer excels. He approaches the catchphrase-creating process with the focused verve of a pop songwriter. He generates constantly, testing which ones work. He seeks snappy, visceral phrases that use vivid images to help team members connect. Richard Coraine's office contains a whiteboard that is covered with works in progress.

We are all paid to solve problems. Make sure to pick
  fun people to solve problems with.
There's glory in making a mistake.
Stone after stone to form a bridge.

Meyer's not alone. Many leaders of high-proficiency
groups focus on creating priorities, naming keystone behaviors, and flooding the environment with heuristics that link
the two. For example, if you spend time around the New
Zealand All-Blacks rugby team, you will hear them talk about
"leaving the jersey in a better place," and saying, "If you're
not growing anywhere, you're not going anywhere," keeping a "blue head" instead of a "red head" (which refers to
calmness under pressure), "Pressure is a privilege," "TQB—
total quality ball," "KBA—keep the ball alive," "Front up,
or fuck off," "It's an honor, not a job," "Go for the gap,"
and "Better people make better All-Blacks."

KIPP, the network of highly successful charter schools, is
similarly built around catchphrases like "No shortcuts,"
"Work hard, be nice," "Don't eat the marshmallow," "Team
and family," "If there's a problem, we look for the solution," "Read, baby, read," "All of us will learn," "KIPPsters
do the right thing when no one is watching," "Everything is
earned," "Be the constant, not the variable," "If a teammate
needs help, we give; if we need help, we ask," "No robots,"
and "Prove the doubters wrong."

At first encounter, a heuristic-dense culture feels slightly
off-putting. "For the first few days I worked here, I heard all
the language, and it was like, 'Are we in summer camp?'"
says Allison Staad, Shake Shack's senior marketing and

communications manager. "It's totally hokey and corny. And then you start to see how they work, and you start using them in regular life. Then all of a sudden they're not corny—they're just part of the oxygen."

"The most powerful thing about all those phrases is the way Danny embodies them," says Coraine. "What he's exceptional at is realizing that people are looking at him every second, and he's delivering those messages every second, every day. He's like a powerful Wi-Fi signal. Some people send three bars, but Danny is at ten bars, and he never goes below nine."

16   How to Lead for Creativity

On a fundamental level, Danny Meyer, KIPP, and the All-Blacks are using the same purpose-building technique. We might call it the lighthouse method: They create purpose by generating a clear beam of signals that link A (where we are) to B (where we want to be). There's another dimension of leadership, however, where the goal isn't to get from A to B but to navigate to an unknown destination, X. This is the dimension of creativity and innovation.

Creative leadership appears to be mysterious, because we tend to regard creativity as a gift, as a quasi-magical ability to see things that do not yet exist and to invent them. Accordingly, we tend to think of creative leaders as artists, able to tap into wellsprings of inspiration and genius that are inaccessible to the rest of us. And to be sure, some leaders fit this description.

The funny thing is, when I visited leaders of successful creative cultures, I didn't meet many artists. Instead, I met a different type, a type who spoke quietly and tended to spend a lot of time observing, who had an introverted vibe and liked to talk about systems. I started to think of this type of person as a Creative Engineer.

Ed Catmull is such a leader. A soft-spoken seventy-two-year-old with a bristly beard and quick, watchful eyes, he is president and cofounder of Pixar, one of the most successful creative cultures of all time. Every other studio in the world hopes to create a hit once in a while. Pixar can be thought of as a machine that creates hits every single time. Since 1995, it has made seventeen feature films, which have earned an average of more than half a billion dollars, won thirteen Academy Awards, and generated some of the most beloved cultural touchstones of our age. A decade ago Catmull took a side job of co-leading Walt Disney Animation Studios and helped it generate a string of blockbusters including *Frozen*, *Big Hero 6*, and *Zootopia*.

I meet Catmull at Pixar's headquarters in Emeryville, California, inside the studio's sleek Brooklyn building. Brooklyn, built in 2010, is a sunlit box of glass and reclaimed wood, brimming with Pixarian touches like a speakeasy, a fireplace, a full-service café, and a roof deck. It is easily one of the most stunning office buildings I've ever seen. (As one early visitor put it, "Thanks for ruining the rest of my life.") As Catmull and I walk through shafts of sunlight, I make a passing remark about the building's beauty.

He stops and turns to face me. His voice is quiet and authoritative, the voice of a doctor making a diagnosis: "In fact, this building was a mistake."

I lean in, unsure I've heard correctly.

"The reason it's a mistake," Catmull continues evenly, "is that it doesn't create the kinds of interactions we need to create. We should have made the hallways wider. We should have made the café bigger, to draw more people. We should have put the offices around the edges to create more shared space in the center. So it wasn't like there was one mistake. There were really a lot of mistakes, along of course with the bigger mistake that we didn't see most of the mistakes until it was too late."

This is an unusual thing for a president of a company to say. If you compliment most leaders on their beautiful multimillion-dollar building, they say thank you, and they mean it. Most leaders will not admit mistakes of this magnitude because they feel the admission would produce a dangerous whiff of incompetence. But not Catmull. He loves these moments; in a way, he lives for them. There is no blame or judgment in his gaze, only a quiet satisfaction born of clarity. *We made some mistakes with this building, and now we know that, and we are slightly better because we know that.*

If you set out to design a life that represented the perfect merger of art and science, you might design one that looks like Catmull's. The child of educators, he spent his early years idolizing Einstein and Disney, studying drawing and physics, and dreaming of making feature-length animated movies. After college, he landed a job with George Lucas, which led to a partnership with Steve Jobs and the creation of Pixar, a small studio with ambitions of fusing computers and filmmaking.

For several years, Pixar struggled. Then in 1995 came the breakthrough, the $360 million success of *Toy Story*. That's when Catmull began to get a nagging feeling that something was out of balance. He knew that other companies had been in this precise situation—on top of the world, flush with cash, lauded for their creativity and innovation. And most of them had stumbled, lost their way, and collapsed. The question was why? And how could Pixar avoid that fate? Catmull talked about that moment in a podcast.

"So the question was, okay, how do you make it so that it's sustainable? Because the people I knew of who were in these [failed] companies—and I had a lot of friends in Silicon Valley—were smart, and they were creative, and they were hardworking. So whatever problem was actually leading them astray was really hard to see, and the implication was, whatever that force was, it would also apply to us at Pixar. So this became the interesting question. These forces are at work—can we find them before they do us in? So at the end of the year I realized that this is actually the next goal. It's not a film. It's how we can have an environment where we can find and address these problems."

We leave the Brooklyn building and walk across campus to the Steve Jobs building, which possesses many of the features Brooklyn lacks: a massive and welcoming central atrium, wide hallways for congregation, and a hivelike buzz. Near the stairs on the second floor stand two offices that embody the two pillars of Pixar's creative approach. The office on the left belongs to John Lasseter, Pixar's creative compass, master storyteller, and muse. His office is almost invisible beneath a Day-Glo moraine of toys: action figures, dolls, both old and new, dozens of versions of Mickey Mouse, Woody, and Buzz Lightyear. On the right is Catmull's office, looking as if it were lifted intact from a German aerospace firm: cool, efficient rectangles rendered in black, white, and gray.

Catmull sits down and starts explaining, in his calm doctorly voice, how Pixar's creativity happens. "All the movies are bad at first," he says. "Some are beyond bad. *Frozen* and *Big Hero 6,* for instance, were unmitigated disasters. The stories were flat, the characters weren't there. They sucked. I'm not saying that in a modest way. I was in the meetings. I saw the early versions, and they were bad. Really bad."

This pattern is not unusual at Pixar. In the original *Toy Story,* Woody started out as bossy and unlikable ("a sarcastic jerk," Catmull says). The early versions of *Up* were so bad that the entire story was changed. "Literally the only thing that stayed the same was the word *up,*" he says.

When most people tell stories about their successful creative endeavors, those stories often go like this: *The project started out as a complete disaster, but then at the last moment, somehow we managed to rescue it.* This arc is attractive because it dramatizes the improbability of the rescue and thus places the teller in a flattering light. But Catmull is doing something profoundly different. He sees the disaster and the rescue not as improbable companions but as causally related. The fact that these projects start out as painful, frustrating disasters is not an accident but a necessity. This is because all creative projects are cognitive puzzles involving thousands of choices and thousands of potential ideas, and you almost never get the right answer right away. Building purpose in a creative group is not about generating a brilliant moment of breakthrough but rather about building systems that can churn through lots of ideas in order to help unearth the right choices.

This is why Catmull has learned to focus less on the ideas

than on people—specifically, on providing teams with tools and support to locate paths, make hard choices, and navigate the arduous process together. "There's a tendency in our business, as in all businesses, to value the idea as opposed to the person or a team of people," he says. "But that's not accurate. Give a good idea to a mediocre team, and they'll find a way to screw it up. Give a mediocre idea to a good team, and they'll find a way to make it better. The goal needs to be to get the team right, get them moving in the right direction, and get them to see where they are making mistakes and where they are succeeding."

I ask Catmull how he knows when a team is succeeding.

"Mostly you can feel it in the room," he says. "When a team isn't working, you see defensive body language, or you see people close down. Or there's just silence. The ideas stop coming, or they can't see the problems. We used to use Steve [Jobs] as a kind of a two-by-four to whack people in the head so they could see the problems in the movie—Steve was good at that.

"But it becomes harder and harder as time goes on, because as directors get more experience, they sometimes have a harder time hearing other points of view that might help them. There are so many parts you have to get right, and it's so easy to get lost in this swirling mass. Your first conclusions are always wrong, and so are your second and your third. So you have to create mechanisms where teams of people can keep working together to see what's really happening and then work together to solve the problems."

Pixar realizes these mechanisms in a set of regular organizational habits. In the Dailies, held in the morning, all of

Pixar's people gather to view and comment on the previous day's footage. (Animation is a spectacularly slow process; each day produces only a few seconds of film.) In field trips, teams immerse themselves in the environments of their movies (scuba-diving trips for the *Finding Nemo* team; archery lessons for the *Brave* team; cooking lessons for the *Ratatouille* team). In BrainTrust meetings (discussed in Chapter 7) a team of Pixar's top storytellers provides regular, vigorously candid, and painful feedback on films in development. At Pixar University, an assortment of classes acts as a kind of mixer, allowing people from different areas of the company to learn side by side. (The classes teach everything from fencing to painting to tai chi.) And in the postmortems, off-site retreats that Catmull organizes after a film is completed, the team members capture and share the biggest takeaways from the process.

Each gathering brings team members together in a safe, flat, high-candor environment and lets them point out problems and generate ideas that move the team, stepwise, toward a better solution. (Not surprisingly, Catmull is a passionate admirer of the Japanese concept of *kaizen,* or continual improvement.) Most of these meetings access the brainpower of the entire group while maintaining the creative team's ownership over the project.*

---

* You see this pattern with many highly creative groups, such as Lockheed's famous Skunk Works (which designed the U-2, the Blackbird, the Nighthawk, and several other legendary planes in record time), Xerox's PARC (which invented the computer interface that Steve Jobs "borrowed" for Apple), Google X, Procter & Gamble's Clay Street, and Mattel's Project Platypus, all of which are essentially the same place: physically distant from the parent group, nonhierarchical, and given maximum autonomy.

Accordingly, Catmull has almost no direct involvement with creative decisions. This is because he realizes that (1) the teams are in a better position to solve problems, and (2) a suggestion from a powerful person tends to be followed. One of his frequently used phrases is "Now it's up to you." This is also why he tends to let a troubled project roll on "a bit too long," as he puts it, before pulling the plug and/or restarting it with a different team. "If you do a restart before everyone is completely ready, you risk upsetting things," he says. "You have to wait until it's clear to everyone that it needs to be restarted."

Catmull is congenitally wary of mottoes and catchphrases, as he believes they can easily distort reality. Nonetheless a handful of "Ed-isms" are heard in Pixar's corridors. Here are a few:

Hire people smarter than you.
Fail early, fail often.
Listen to everyone's ideas.
Face toward the problems.
B-level work is bad for your soul.
It's more important to invest in good people than in
  good ideas.

You'll notice that, in contrast to Danny Meyer's vivid, specific language, these are defiantly un-catchy, almost zen-like in their plainness and universality. This reflects the fundamental difference between leading for proficiency and leading for creativity: Meyer needs people to know and feel exactly what to do, while Catmull needs people to discover that for themselves.

Catmull spends his days roving around Pixar and Disney, watching. He helps onboard new employees and observes BrainTrust meetings, hawkeyeing the interactions for signs of incipient trouble or success. He cultivates back-channel conversations to find out what's going on behind the scenes. He worries when he sees awkward silences or people avoiding each other; he celebrates when a group takes initiative without asking permission (such as when a group of animators organized an impromptu Boy Scout–themed sleepover on Pixar's lawn). He defends teams when they make mistakes (and they can make some extremely expensive mistakes).

If Danny Meyer is a lighthouse, beaming signals of purpose, then Catmull is more like the engineer of a ship. Catmull doesn't steer the ship—he roves around belowdecks, checking the hull for leaks, changing out a piston, adding a little oil here and there. "For me, managing is a creative act," he says. "It's problem solving, and I love doing that."

If you were to create a field experiment to test Catmull's leadership methods, it might consist of the following steps: (1) locate a struggling movie studio; (2) place Catmull in charge and, without changing any personnel, allow him to reengineer the group's culture. Then you would wait to see what happened.

That, in fact, is precisely what happened in 2006. The struggling studio happened to be Walt Disney Animation.

After a run of success in the 1990s, Disney had entered a decade-long creative wasteland, producing a series of films that were consistently flat and dull and, not coincidentally, unprofitable. (This string included *The Lost Empire, Brother Bear, Treasure Planet,* and *Home on the Range,* which featured a burping cow voiced by Roseanne Barr.) So Disney CEO Bob Iger attempted the corporate equivalent of a heart transplant, purchasing Pixar and putting Catmull and Lasseter in charge of reviving the most storied brand in animation—and maybe in all of entertainment.

Most observers didn't expect the combination to work out. For starters, there was the size differential. Pixar was relatively small, while Disney was gargantuan, and it was hard to imagine that Catmull and Lasseter could control it. "Like Nemo swallowing the whale" was the way *Fortune* magazine put it. Another factor was the geographic challenge: Pixar was in Emeryville, near Oakland, while Disney was 350 miles away in Burbank. Entertainment-industry history showed that these kinds of acquisitions were risky and often harmful to both parties.

After the sale went through, Catmull and Lasseter traveled to Burbank and made a speech to Disney employees. Lasseter was inspiring, talking about legacy and rejuvenation. Catmull, typically, said about two sentences. "We're not going to turn Disney into a clone of Pixar. What we're going to do is build a studio on your talent and passion."

They got to work, starting with physical structure. At the time of the acquisition, Disney employees were scattered across four floors of a giant building, siloed in groups that reflected their expertise (animation, layout, design) rather than their collaborative function. Catmull headed up a rebuild that smooshed all the creative and technical people together around a central gathering place called the Caffeine Patch. He then put his and Lasseter's offices (they committed to spending two days a week at Disney) near the center.

Next Catmull focused on creative structure. Disney had been using the conventional film development model, which worked as follows: (1) studio executives create development teams, which are charged with generating stories; (2) studio executives evaluate those ideas, decide which would be developed, and assign directors to each one; (3) directors make the movies, and executives evaluate early versions, offer notes, and occasionally create competitions called "bake-offs" to decide which film is ready for release.

Catmull flipped that system on its head, removing creative power from the executives and placing it in the hands of the directors. In the new structure, the directors were responsible for coming up with their own ideas and pitching them, rather than being assigned them by studio executives. The job of the executives was not to be all-deciding bosses but rather to support the directors and their teams as they undertook the painful journey from idea to workable concept to finished film. Early in the transition, Catmull invited Disney directors and executives to Pixar to observe a Brain-Trust meeting. They watched the team work together to pick a movie apart and do the hard work of rebuilding it.

The change in the energy at Disney was immediate. Disney directors called it a breath of fresh air and likened it to the fall of the Berlin Wall. It was a moment of hope, reinforced by the fact that the Disney team's subsequent movie improvement meetings (they dubbed them the Story Trust) were judged to be the best and most useful anyone there had experienced.

Catmull, however, wasn't as quick to celebrate, knowing that real change wasn't going to happen overnight. "It takes time," he says. "You have to go through some failures and some screw-ups, and survive them, and support each other through them. And then after that happens, you really begin to trust one another."

Which is what happened. The first few films after the acquisition were immediately better, scoring improved reviews as well as box office success. Then in 2010, Disney's teams began clicking at a Pixarian level, with *Tangled* ($591 million in worldwide box office), *Wreck-It Ralph* ($471 million), *Frozen* ($1.2 billion), *Big Hero 6* ($657 million), and *Zootopia* ($931 million). Catmull notes that the transformation happened with virtually no turnover. "The people who made these films are the same people who were there when they were failing," he says. "We put in some new systems, they learned new ways of interacting, and they changed their behavior, and now they are a completely different group of people when they work together."

We put in some new systems, and they learned new ways of interacting. It's strange to think that a wave of creativity and innovation can be unleashed by something as mundane as changing systems and learning new ways of interacting. But it's true, because building creative purpose isn't really about creativity. It's about building ownership, providing support, and aligning group energy toward the arduous, error-filled, ultimately fulfilling journey of making something new.

Ideas for Action

Here's a surprising fact about successful cultures: many were forged in moments of crisis. Pixar's crisis occurred in 1998 when it set out to make a straight-to-video sequel to the highly acclaimed *Toy Story*. The studio embarked on the project presuming it would be a relatively simple process—after all, how hard could a sequel be? But early versions were awful. The story lacked emotion, the characters were flat, and the film lacked the sparkle and heart of the original. Catmull and Lasseter realized this was a question of Pixar's core purpose. Was it a studio that did average work or one that aimed for greatness? At their urging, Pixar scrapped the early versions and started over at the eleventh hour, aiming for a full theatrical release instead of video. This successful last-minute push crystallized Pixar's identity and resulted in the invention of many of its signature collaborative systems (including the BrainTrust).

The SEALs experienced a similar moment in 1983, during the invasion of Grenada. The mission had been straightforward: One team would parachute into the sea, swim to shore, and capture Grenada's only radio antenna. Unfortunately, a combination of weather, poor communication, and bad decisions led to the team being dropped at night in a storm, overloaded with gear. The result was the drowning deaths of four SEALs—and a subsequent rebuilding of the group's decision-making and communications systems.

Danny Meyer's early days as a restaurateur, too, were punctuated by a string of near-disasters. "We nearly killed a customer when a light fixture fell out of a wall," he says. "Another time I got into a fistfight with a customer who'd had too much to drink. And I'm not talking just a shoving match. It was a real fistfight in front of the whole restaurant. He punched me in the jaw and slammed my head in a door, and I kicked him in the nuts. Let's just say that we're lucky that the Internet didn't exist in those days."

The difference with successful cultures seems to be that they use the crisis to crystallize their purpose. When leaders of those groups reflect on those failures now, they express gratitude (and sometimes even nostalgic desire) for those moments, as painful as they were, because they were the crucible that helped the group discover what it could be.

This gives us insight into building purpose. It's not as simple as carving a mission statement in granite or encouraging everyone to recite from a hymnal of catchphrases. It's a never-ending process of trying, failing, reflecting, and above all, learning. High-purpose environments don't descend on groups from on high; they are dug out of the ground, over and over, as a group navigates its problems together and evolves to meet the challenges of a fast-changing world.

Here are a few ideas to help you do that.

Name and Rank Your Priorities: In order to move toward a target, you must first have a target. Listing your priorities, which means wrestling with the choices that define your identity, is the first step. Most successful groups end up with a small handful of priorities (five or fewer), and many, not coincidentally, end up placing their in-group relationships—how they treat one another—at the top of the list. This reflects the truth that many successful groups realize: Their greatest project is building and sustaining the group itself. If they get their own relationships right, everything else will follow.

Be Ten Times as Clear About Your Priorities as You Think You Should Be: A while back *Inc.* magazine asked executives at six hundred companies to estimate the percentage of their workforce who could name the company's top three priorities. The executives predicted that 64 percent would be able to name them. When *Inc.* then asked employees to name the priorities, only 2 percent could do so. This is not the exception but the rule. Leaders are inherently biased to presume that everyone in the group sees things as they do, when in fact they don't. This is why it's necessary to drastically overcommunicate priorities. The leaders I visited with were not shy about this. Statements of priorities were painted on walls, stamped on emails, incanted in speeches, dropped into conversation, and repeated over and over until they became part of the oxygen.

One way to create awareness is to make a habit of regularly testing the company's values and purpose, as James Burke did with the Credo challenge. This involves creating conversations that encourage people to grapple with the big questions: *What are we about? Where are we headed?* Many of the leaders I met seemed to do this instinctively, cultivating what might be called a productive dissatisfaction. They were mildly suspicious of success. They presumed that there were other, better ways of doing things, and they were unafraid of change. They presumed they didn't have all the answers and so constantly sought guidance and clarity.

Figure Out Where Your Group Aims for Proficiency and Where It Aims for Creativity: Every group skill can be sorted into one of two basic types: skills of proficiency and skills of creativity.

Skills of proficiency are about doing a task the same way, every single time. They are about delivering machine-like reliability, and they tend to apply in domains in which the goal behaviors are clearly defined, such as service. Building purpose to perform these skills is like building a vivid map: You want to spotlight the goal and provide crystal-clear directions to the checkpoints along the way. Ways to do that include:

- Fill the group's windshield with clear, accessible models of excellence.
- Provide high-repetition, high-feedback training.
- Build vivid, memorable rules of thumb (*if* X, *then* Y).
- Spotlight and honor the fundamentals of the skill.

Creative skills, on the other hand, are about empowering a group to do the hard work of building something that has never existed before. Generating purpose in these areas is like supplying an expedition: You need to provide support, fuel, and tools and to serve as a protective presence that empowers the team doing the work. Some ways to do that include:

- Keenly attend to team composition and dynamics.
- Define, reinforce, and relentlessly protect the team's creative autonomy.
- Make it safe to fail and to give feedback.
- Celebrate hugely when the group takes initiative.

Most groups, of course, consist of a combination of these skill types, as they aim for proficiency in certain areas and creativity in others. The key is to clearly identify these areas and tailor leadership accordingly.

Embrace the Use of Catchphrases: When you look at successful groups, a lot of their internal language features catchphrases that often sound obvious, rah-rah, or corny. Many of us instinctively dismiss them as cultish jargon. But this is a mistake. Their occasionally cheesy obviousness is not a bug—it's a feature. Their clarity, grating to the outsider's ear, is precisely what helps them function.

The trick to building effective catchphrases is to keep them simple, action-oriented, and forthright: "Create fun and a little weirdness" (Zappos), "Talk less, do more" (IDEO), "Work hard, be nice" (KIPP), "Pound the rock" (San Antonio Spurs), "Leave the jersey in a better place" (New Zealand All-Blacks), "Create raves for guests" (Danny Meyer's restaurants). They're hardly poetry, but they share an action-based clarity. They aren't gentle suggestions so much as clear reminders, crisp nudges in the direction the group wants to go.

Measure What Really Matters: The main challenge to building a clear sense of purpose is that the world is cluttered with noise, distractions, and endless alternative purposes. One solution is to create simple universal measures that place focus on what matters. A good example happened in the early days of Zappos, when Tony Hsieh noticed that call center workers were measured by the number of calls they handled per hour. He realized that this traditional measure was at odds with the group's purpose and that it was driving unwanted behaviors (haste and brevity, for starters). So he banished that metric and replaced it with Personal Emotional Connections (PECs), or creating a bond outside the conversation about the product. It's impossible, of course, to measure PECs precisely, but the goal here is not precision; it is to create awareness and alignment and to direct behavior toward the group's mission. So when a customer service agent spent a company-record 10 hours and 29 minutes on a call, Zappos celebrated and sent out a press release.*

Use Artifacts: If you traveled from Mars to Earth to visit successful cultures, it would not take you long to figure out

---

* The call covered a wide variety of subjects, including movies, favorite foods, and what it's like to live in Las Vegas. It resulted in the sale of one pair of Ugg boots.

what they were about. Their environments are richly embedded with artifacts that embody their purpose and identity. These artifacts vary widely: the battle gear of soldiers killed in combat at the Navy SEAL headquarters; the Oscar trophies accompanied by hand-drawn sketches of the original concepts at Pixar; and the rock and sledgehammer behind glass at the San Antonio Spurs practice facility, embodying the team's catchphrase "Pound the rock"—but they all reinforce the same signal: *This is what matters*.

Focus on Bar-Setting Behaviors: One challenge of building purpose is to translate abstract ideas (values, mission) into concrete terms. One way successful groups do this is by spotlighting a single task and using it to define their identity and set the bar for their expectations.

One good example is the men's hockey team at Quinnipiac University, a small school in Hamden, Connecticut. The team fields few highly recruited players, yet it has spent the last half-decade as one of the nation's top-ranked teams. Quinnipiac's coach, Rand Pecknold, has built a culture around a specific behavior he calls "Forty for Forty." The phrase refers to back-checking, which means rushing back to the defensive end in response to the other team's attack—basically, chasing them down. Back-checking happens around forty times per game, and it is Pecknold's goal that his players go all-out with 100 percent effort on each one—in other words, Forty for Forty. It is not easy to do. Back-checking is exhausting, requires keen attentiveness, and—here's the key—rarely makes a difference in the game.

"It almost never pays off," Pecknold says. "You can back-check thirty-nine times in a row, and it doesn't make any difference at all in the play. But the fortieth time, maybe something happens. You get a stick in, you steal the puck, you stop a goal, or you create a turnover that leads to a goal. That one back-check doesn't show up anywhere in the stat books, but it can change a game. That's why we are Forty for Forty. That's who we are."

Quinnipiac team members talk about Forty for Forty all the time. They talk about it during practice, during games, and during Pecknold's regular one-on-one meetings with players. And on those rare moments when a successful back-check happens in a game, Pecknold spotlights the moment.

"The next day I get it on video, and I set it all up," he says. "I'm not one to drop f-bombs a lot with the team—you gotta be really careful where you do that. But I do it here. I'll cue up the tape of the back-check and set it up like it's a movie. I'll say, 'Watch Shutty [forward Tommy Shutt] right here. Look at fucking Shutty go. Look at him take this guy out.' And everybody goes nuts. Even if Shutty's back-check leads to a goal, I never talk about the guy who scored the goal or the guy who had the assist—they don't even exist. All I talk about is Shutty and this great back-check, and how it happened because we were Forty for Forty. You can see all the guys feeling it, and the next time we practice, everybody is on it, doing it, loving it."

Pecknold is not the only leader to build purpose around spotlighting a small, effortful behavior. At his restaurants, Danny Meyer is known for moving the salt shaker if it shifts even slightly from its spot at the table's center. Teachers at

KIPP Infinity in Harlem still talk about how founder Dave Levin would place each student's water bottle in millimeter-accurate arrangement with their notebooks on the first day of school. Pixar puts hundreds of hours of effort into the technical and storytelling quality of the short, stand-alone animated films that run before each of its features. The shorts lose money, but they pay off in other ways. They invest in the studio's young talent, create experimentation, and most important, showcase the attention and excellence they channel into every task. In other words, these small efforts are powerful because they transmit, amplify, and celebrate the purpose of the whole group.

Writing a book, like every journey, leaves a person changed. As I worked on this project over the past four years, I found myself noticing subtle moments of connection that I had previously missed. I appreciated how certain places—the local bakery, my children's school, the gas station—used small interactions to build a cohesive culture. I found myself admiring leaders who opened up about their shortcomings to create honest conversations. At home, I parented a little differently: I talked less and focused more on seeking ways to create belonging. (Card games are the absolute best.) It wasn't as if I were suddenly graced with X-ray vision; it was more like learning a sport. First you are clumsy; then after a while, you get better.

One place I used these skills most was in coaching a team. It wasn't a sports team but a team of writers at the Ruffing Montessori middle school in Cleveland Heights, Ohio, which my two youngest daughters attended. The writing team competed in Power of the Pen, a statewide competition. Students practice all year for a one-day tournament at which they are given three short prompts ("Keeping the Secret," say, or "Buried Treasure") to produce three stories, which judges then score and rank. It's a fun and inspiring event, because it combines the creativity of writing with the scoreboard adrenaline of sports.

It's also an event at which Ruffing had historically struggled. In the previous decade (I'd been coaching for two years), its students had occasionally advanced past the first-round tournament but rarely got much further. This result made sense—after all, Ruffing is tiny, consisting of only forty students, competing against Goliath-size schools from around the state. But it made me wonder if our team could do better. So in 2014, as an experiment, I decided to apply some ideas from the research for this book.

Our first weekly practice session in October drew nine students. Catherine, Carson, Ellie, Vala, Caroline, Natsumi, David, Nathan, and Zoe were an energetic group with a range of skill levels and motivations. Vala and Ellie were confident and experienced writers, while Carson and Caroline were more hesitant, just starting to stretch their creative muscles. I was hesitant, too. In years past, I'd taken a traditional (i.e., authoritative) approach to coaching the team: I did a lot of speaking, gave lecture-like talks, then provided feedback on their practice stories. In teaching parlance, I was "the sage on the stage," and it was a comfortable place to stand. This year, however, would be different.

First, I changed the seating arrangement. In years past we had sat in loose proximity at a scattering of small tables. Now I shoved four small tables together to form one table just big enough to fit the ten of us, elbow to elbow. Then, rather than launching into a lecture about good writing, I asked the team, "What's your favorite book right now?" We went around the circle. (Harry Potter made more than one appearance, as did *Hunger Games*.)

Then I asked why those books were so good.

"Because he's an orphan," Ellie said. "Pretty much every good story has orphans."

"Because there's an intense war happening," Nathan said. "All these people are dying, and it's brutal and you don't want them to die."

"Because it's just really, really good," Carson said.

"Why?" I asked.

Carson swallowed. He was a tall, slender kid, with large dark eyes and a formal manner. He chose his words carefully. "Because the story makes you worry about them," he said.

"Yes," I said. I gave him a fist bump, and he smiled.

I asked the team another question: "What do you *not* like about writing?"

Answers came fast: They didn't like coming up with ideas to write about. Sometimes stories came easily, but often they didn't, and they were left staring at a blank page, wondering what to write about.

"I just get stuck sometimes," Catherine said, speaking for the group. "I get partway, and then I can't think of anything."

I told the team I had something to share with them. I reached into my backpack and, with a shamelessly dramatic flourish, produced a stack of paper—early drafts of this book. They took the sheets eagerly. They knew I was a writer, and they were expecting to find examples of faultless prose.

But as they read, they saw that the pages weren't perfect. To the contrary, they were riddled with handwritten edits, line-outs, and fixes scribbled in the margins. Entire pages had been crossed out. It didn't look like the work of a published writer. It looked like a school assignment that had earned a resounding F.

"This is yours?" Nathan asked.

"Yes," I said.

"Are there this many changes every time?" Vala asked.

"Every time," I said.

I told them that nothing I ever wrote was perfect; that I often got stuck and struggled through the process of building a story. I told them I tended to make lots of mistakes and that noticing and fixing those mistakes was where the writing improved.

Then I gave the team a prompt. After they'd written for fifteen minutes, I asked them to put their pens down and explained a simple rule: Everyone was encouraged to read their story aloud, and everyone was encouraged to give feedback. Some of the students were hesitant about reading their stories aloud, and they lacked the language to critique other stories. But slowly, as weeks passed, we got better. Caroline, who hadn't wanted to read her stories at first, started to share more openly, bringing us into the sci-fi worlds she liked to create. Natsumi, initially hesitant about offering criticism to her teammates, started weighing in with warm, pointed guidance.

We adopted a "What Worked Well/Even Better If" format for the feedback sessions: first celebrating the story's positives, then offering ideas for improvement. Over time the

exchanges strengthened into habits; the group stopped behaving like a typical class and started behaving like the kindergartners in the spaghetti-marshmallow challenge: working
shoulder to shoulder, fixing problems, thinking as one.

Meanwhile I focused on supporting those interactions.
When someone wrote a successful story or offered a particularly incisive comment, I didn't say a word but rather gave a
fist bump. Like Danny Meyer, I flooded the zone with catchphrases to guide them through the writing-and-fixing process. One was "Power of the Problem," which reminded
them that most effective stories consist of characters struggling with huge problems, the bigger, the better. (After all,
Captain Ahab doesn't chase minnows.) Another was "Use
Your Camera," which reminded them to control the point
of view. (Do you want to take the reader inside the character's mind, or to observe them from above?) I told them over
and over: "Every story should have VOW: voice, obstacles,
and wanting. The bigger the problem, the better the story.
You guys are creative athletes—you have to help each other
get better."

For me, in some ways, this coaching style was more demanding. It required more reflection, thinking about ways
to ignite discussion and to motivate. I also struggled with
the challenge of *not* doing things: allowing conversations to
occasionally ramble off-topic instead of leaping in to seize
control. In other ways, however, the new style was easier.
Instead of focusing on conveying knowledge (which demanded lots of preparation and precision), I could serve as
a guide, letting the group function, watching for moments
where I could step in and, with a phrase or body language,

create some awareness or, better, highlight a successful choice they had made.

The district tournament took place on Valentine's Day. That morning a blizzard descended on northeastern Ohio, delivering five inches of snow and forty-four-mile-per-hour winds. We drove to the host school through the storm, catching glimpses of cars and semis spun off the road, emergency services workers huddled by the roadside, in a roaring moonscape of white that looked like the zombie apocalypse. "We should write a story about this storm," Zoe said, and the rest of the team started weaving narratives from the images they saw.

When we arrived at the host school, we found a table near the window. Then the kids bumped fists and disappeared into classrooms to receive their prompts and write their stories. Two hours later they emerged, wide-eyed and wrung out. At three o'clock, after scoring and ranking all the pieces, the tournament organizers ushered us, along with several hundred other competitors, into the gym to announce the winners.

Long story short: We did well. In the seventh-grade division, Zoe finished fourteenth. In the eighth-grade division, Nathan finished twelfth, Vala tenth, Natsumi fourth, and Ellie first. By day's end, we were lifting the first-place trophy for eighth grade. A few weeks later the team performed similarly well in another district tournament, where Zoe won first place and best of round. Four students qualified for states, the most in the school's history, and Ellie won an award for talented young writers.

But for me that was not the highlight. The highlight involved Carson, the quiet eighth-grader who had never done much writing. While he did not advance past the district tournament, he kept showing up at Tuesday practice sessions. He wasn't so shy anymore about sharing his writing, and he was showing his creativity in other ways. (That spring, to the surprise of teachers and parents, he would perform a terrific Atticus Finch in the school's production of *To Kill a Mockingbird*.)

On the team, Carson's specialty was writing comic stories about a legendary character named Johnny McTough, a tall, handsome, titanically confident high schooler who was under the misimpression that he was the greatest football player in the world. Johnny McTough stories were wonderful partly because Johnny's unshakable belief that he didn't need anyone—not a coach, not a team, not his parents, not even a helmet—led him into all kinds of funny predicaments. But mostly they were wonderful because of the way Carson and the team interacted. Each week, in a swaggering, macho voice, Carson would relate Johnny McTough's latest adventure, and the team would laugh uproariously. We would laugh at the spectacle of this misguided hero who thought he could take on the world alone. Then we would all start working together to make that story even better.

Acknowledgments

Writing this book was a team project, and I am lucky to have some exceptionally skilled coaches. Foremost among them are Andy Ward, my brilliant editor, and David Black, my superb agent.

My brother Maurice is an incredibly talented editor and writer, and was invaluable throughout the research and writing process, creating concepts, challenging ideas, editing manuscripts, and patiently engaging in hundreds of conversations. Those conversations, more than any others, are where this book took its shape.

At Random House, I'd like to thank Kaela Myers, Cindy Murray, Susan Corcoran, Kim Hovey, Kara Walsh, Sanyu Dillon, Debbie Aroff, Theresa Zoro, Max Minckler, Scott Shannon, Simon Sullivan, Amelia Zalcman, Paolo Pepe, and Gina Centrello. At Black Inc: Susan Raihofer, Emily Hoffman, Sarah Smith, and Jenny Herrera. At Wanashaker: Margaret Ewen, Kathryn Ewen, and Adrienne Zand. At Pixar: Ed Catmull, Michelle Radcliff, Wendy Tanzillo, and Mike Sundy. At the San Antonio Spurs: R. C. Buford, Chip Engelland, Chad Forcier, and Sean Marks. At Zappos: Maggie Hsu, Joe Mahon, Lisa Shufro, Angel Sugg, Jeanne Markel, Zubin Damania, Zach Ware, and Connie Yeh. At IDEO: Duane Bray, Nili Metuki, Njoki Gitahi, Lawrence Abrahamson, Peter Antonelli, and Nadia Walker. At KIPP: Dave Levin, Mike Feinberg, Joe Negron, Allison Willis Holley, Lauren Abramson, Angela Fascilla, Jeff Li, Carly Scott, Alexa Roche, and Glenn

Davis. At the Upright Citizens Brigade: Kevin Hines and Nate Dern. At Union Square Hospitality Group: Danny Meyer, Erin Moran, Haley Carroll, Richard Coraine, Rachel Hoffheimer, Susan Reilly Salgado, Stephanie Jackson, Kim DiPalo, Allison Staad, and Tanya Edmunds. I'd also like to thank the members of the Navy SEAL community who prefer not to be named here.

Many within the scientific community gave of their time and expertise. I'd like to especially thank Jay Van Bavel, Amy Edmondson, Sigal Barsade, Gregory Walton, Geoff Cohen, Jeff Polzer, Carl Marci, Will Felps, Tom Allen, Jeffry Simpson, Clifford Stott, Andy Molinsky, Bradley Staats, Oren Lederman, Alex Pentland, Reb Rebele, Constantinos Coutifaris, Matthew Corritore, and Ben Waber.

Many colleagues and friends generously shared insights about group performance and culture—in many cases because they happened to be members of terrific organizations. I'd especially like to thank Chris Antonetti, Mike Chernoff, Terry Francona, Paul and Karen Dolan, Derek Falvey, Carter Hawkins, James Harris, Ceci Clark, Brian Miles, Oscar Gutierrez Ramirez, Alex Eckelman, Eric Binder, Matt Forman, Tom Wiedenbauer, Sky Andrecheck, Victor Wang, Alex Merberg, Matt Blake, Johnny Goryl, Marlene Lehky, Nilda Tafanelli, Ross Atkins, Mark Shapiro, Adam Grant, Peter Vint, John Kessel, Chris Grant, Jerry Azzinaro, Josh Gibson, Steve Gera, Rich Diviney, Sam Presti, Billy Donovan, Mark Daigneault, Oliver Winterbone, Dustin Seale, Scott McLachlan, Mike Forde, Henry Abbott, David Epstein, Alex Gibney, Laszlo Bock, Tom Wujec, Bob Bowman, David Marsh, Finn Gunderson, Richie Graham, Anne Buford, Troy Flanagan, Shawn Hunter, Dennis Jaffe, Rand Pecknold, Brett Ledbetter, Pete Carroll, Cindy Bristow, Michael Ruhlman, Bill Pabst, Jay Berhalter, Nico Romeijn, Wim van Zwam, Scott Flood, Dan Russell, and Doug Lemov.

On the personal side, I'd like to thank Jon Coyle, Marian Jones, John Giuggio, Rob Fisher, Fred and Beeb Fisher, Tom Kizzia, Todd Balf, Jeff and Cindy Keller, Laura Hohnhold, Mike Paterniti, Sara Corbett, Mark Bryant, Marshall Sella, Kathie Freer, Tom and Catie Bursch, Paul Cox, Kirsten Docter, Rob and Emily Pollard, Dave Lucas, George Bilgere, Doug and Lisa Vahey, Carri Thurman, John Rohr, Geo Beach, Sydney Webb, and Lisa Damour for her sharp editor's eye.

Finally, I'd like to thank my parents, Maurice and Agnes Coyle, who have been north stars of inspiration and support from the very start. I'd like to thank my children, Aidan, Katie, Lia, and Zoe, who are the greatest sources of joy and meaning in my life, and who make me incredibly proud. And most of all I'd like to thank my wife, Jen, whose warmth, smarts, and kindness light up every day with love. This book only exists because of you.

Notes

Introduction · When Two Plus Two Equals Ten

For more on culture's effect on the bottom line, see John Kotter and James Heskett's *Corporate Culture and Performance* (New York: The Free Press, 1992); D. Denison and A. Mishra, "Toward a Theory of Organizational Culture and Effectiveness," *Organization Science* 6 (1995), 204–23; and G. Gordon and N. DiTomaso, "Predicting Corporate Performance from Organizational Culture," *Journal of Management Studies* 29 (1992), 783–98.

1 · The Good Apples

For more on belonging cues, see W. Felps, T. Mitchell, and E. Byington, "How, When, and Why Bad Apples Spoil the Barrel: Negative Group Member and Dysfunctional Groups," *Research in Organizational Behavior* 27 (2006), 175–222; J. Curhan and A. Pentland, "Thin Slices of Negotiation: Predicting Outcomes from Conversational Dynamics Within the First Five Minutes," *Journal of Applied Psychology* 92 (2007), 802–11; and William Stoltzman's "Toward a Social Signaling Framework: Activity and Emphasis in Speech," master's thesis, MIT (2006). For an exploration of sociometrics, see Alex Pentland's *Honest Signals* (Cambridge, MA: MIT Press, 2008) and *Social Physics* (New York: The Penguin

Press, 2014) as well as Ben Waber's *People Analytics* (Upper Saddle River, NJ: Pearson FT Press, 2013).

The concept of psychological safety was pioneered by William Kahn in "Psychological Conditions of Personal Engagement and Disengagement at Work," *Academy of Management Journal* 11 (1990), 692–724. Amy Edmondson's work in this area is outstanding; you can find much of it in *Teaming: How Organizations Learn, Innovate, and Compete in the Knowledge Economy* (San Francisco: Jossey-Bass Pfeiffer, 2012).

2 · The Billion-Dollar Day When Nothing Happened

For a deeper look at Google's development of the AdWords engine, see Steven Levy's *In the Plex* (New York: Simon & Schuster, 2011). For more on the success rates of different organizational models, see J. Baron and M. Hannan, "Organizational Blueprints for Success in High-Tech Startups: Lessons from the Stanford Project on Emerging Companies," *California Management Review* 44 (2002), 8–36; and M. Hannan, J. Baron, G. Hsu, and O. Kocak, "Organizational Identities and the Hazard of Change," *Industrial and Corporate Change* 15 (2006), 755–84.

For more on belonging cues and behavior change, see G. Walton, G. Cohen, D. Cwir, and S. Spencer, "Mere Belonging: The Power of Social Connections," *Journal of Personality and Social Psychology* 102 (2012), 513–32; G. Walton and P. Carr, "Social Belonging and the Motivation and Intellectual Achievement of Negatively Stereotyped Students," in *Stereotype Threat: Theory, Processes, and Application,* M. Inzlicht and T. Schmader (eds.) (New York: Oxford University Press, 2012); A. Brooks, H. Dai, and M. Schweitzer, "I'm Sorry About the Rain! Superfluous Apologies Demonstrate Empathic Concern and Increase Trust," *Social*

Psychological and Personality Science 5 (2014), 467–74; G. Carter, K. Clover, I. Whyte, A. Dawson, and C. D'Este, "Postcards from the Edge Project: Randomised Controlled Trial of an Intervention Using Postcards to Reduce Repetition of Hospital Treated Deliberate Self Poisoning," *BMJ* (2005); and P. Fischer, A. Sauer, C. Vogrincic, and S. Weisweiler, "The Ancestor Effect: Thinking about Our Genetic Origin Enhances Intellectual Performance," *European Journal of Social Psychology* 41 (2010), 11–16.

For more on how belonging and identity work inside the brain, see J. Van Bavel, L. Hackel, and Y. Xiao, "The Group Mind: The Pervasive Influence of Social Identity on Cognition," *Research and Perspectives in Neurosciences* 21 (2013), 41–56; D. Packer and J. Van Bavel, "The Dynamic Nature of Identity: From the Brain to Behavior," *The Psychology of Change: Life Contexts, Experiences, and Identities*, N. Branscombe and K. Reynolds (eds.) (Hove, United Kingdom: Psychology Press, 2015); and D. de Cremer and M. van Vugt, "Social Identification Effects in Social Dilemmas," *European Journal of Social Psychology* 29 (1999), 871–93.

3 · The Christmas Truce, the One-Hour Experiment, and the Missileers

The Christmas Truce story has been told in many places; the most in-depth versions can be found in Tony Ashworth's *Trench Warfare 1914–1918: The Live and Let-Live System* (London: Pan Books, 2000) and Stanley Weintraub's *Silent Night* (New York: Plume, 2002). For a wide-angle look at how altruism works, see Robert Axelrod's *The Evolution of Cooperation* (New York: Basic Books, 1984) and Michael Tomasello's *Why We Cooperate* (Cambridge, MA: MIT Press, 2009).

For more on the WIPRO experiment, see D. Cable, F. Gino, and B. Staats, "Breaking Them In or Revealing Their Best? Reframing Socialization Around Newcomer Self-Expression," *Administrative Science Quarterly* 58 (2013), 1–36. For more on the nuclear-launch crews, I'd recommend Eric Schlosser's *Command and Control* (New York: The Penguin Press, 2013).

4 · How to Build Belonging

For Neil Paine's study of Popovich's coaching dominance, see fivethirtyeight.com/features/2014-nba-preview-the-rise-of-the-warriors/. For more on the study of why NBA players tend to behave selfishly, see E. Uhlmann and C. Barnes, "Selfish Play Increases During High-Stakes NBA Games and Is Rewarded with More Lucrative Contracts," *PLoS ONE* 9 (2014).

For more on the magical-feedback study, see D. Yeager, V. Purdie-Vaughns, J. Garcia, N. Apfel, P. Brzustoski, A. Master, W. Hessert, M. Williams, and G. Cohen, "Breaking the Cycle of Mistrust: Wise Interventions to Provide Critical Feedback Across the Racial Divide," *Journal of Experimental Psychology: General* 143 (2013), 804–24.

5 · How to Design for Belonging

For more on Thomas Allen's work, see *Managing the Flow of Technology: Technology Transfer and the Dissemination of Technological Information Within the R&D Organization* (Cambridge, MA: MIT Press, 1984).

Hsieh's urge to MacGyver is still strong. Around the time I visited, he began implementing a radical new management approach called holacracy, which seeks to replace traditional managers with self-organizing "circles" in which people determine their own tasks and roles. To say that holacracy wasn't an immediate success would be to put it mildly. It caused a wave of employee departures, and in 2016 the company failed to make *Fortune* magazine's Top 100 Best Places to Work list for the first time in seven years. Hsieh has since moved to an even more abstract management system called Teal. Whether the organization and the culture can continue to thrive remains to be seen.

6 · Ideas for Action

For more on the power of gratitude, see L. Williams and M. Bartlett, "Warm Thanks: Gratitude Expression Facilitates Social Affiliation in New Relationships via Perceived Warmth," *Emotion* 15 (2014); and A. Grant and F. Gino, "A Little Thanks Goes a Long Way: Explaining Why Gratitude Expressions Motivate Pro-social Behavior," *Journal of Personality and Social Psychology* 98 (2010), 946–55. For more on the shortcomings of sandwich feedback, see C. Von Bergen, M. Bressler, and K. Campbell, "The Sandwich Feedback Method: Not Very Tasty," *Journal of Behavioral Studies in Business* 7 (2014).

Emails are rich repositories of belonging cues; here are two studies that show how they reveal the internal fabric of groups: L. Wu, "Social Network Effects on Productivity and Job Security: Evidence from the Adoption of a Social Networking Tool," *Information Systems Research* 24 (2013), 30–51; and S. Srivastava, A. Goldberg, V. Manian, and C. Potts, "Enculturation Trajectories: Language, Cultural Adaptation, and Individual Outcomes in Organizations," *Management Science*, forthcoming.

7 · "Tell Me What You Want, and I'll Help You"

Flight 232's cockpit voice recording can be found at aviation
-safety.net/investigation/cvr/transcripts/cvr_ua232.pdf. Captain Al
Haynes provided a detailed account of the crash in a May 24,
1991, speech to the NASA Ames Research Center at the Dryden
Flight Research Facility in Edwards, CA, the transcript of which
can be found at clear-prop.org/aviation/haynes.html. In addition,
see *Flight 232* by Laurence Gonzales (New York: W. W. Norton &
Company, 2014) and *Confronting Mistakes* by Jan U. Hagen
(London: Palgrave Macmillan, 2013).

Another element of Flight 232's story involves a set of training
procedures called Crew Resource Management, which had been
established by the National Transportation Safety Board in the
late 1970s after several crashes caused by pilot error. The training
sought to replace the top-down "pilot is always right" culture
with frank, fast communication, teaching captain and crew a series of simple behaviors and habits designed to reveal and solve
problems together. Prior to Flight 232's crash, Captain Haynes
had undergone several weeks of CRM training; he credited the
program for saving his life and that of the other survivors.

8 · The Vulnerability Loop

For more on the science of generating individual and group closeness, see A. Aron, E. Melinat, E. Aron, and R. Bator, "The Experimental Generation of Interpersonal Closeness: A Procedure
and Some Preliminary Findings," *Personality and Social Psychology Bulletin* 23 (1997), 363–77; W. Swann, L. Milton, and J. Polzer, "Should We Create a Niche or Fall in Line? Identity Negotiation
and Small Group Effectiveness," *Journal of Personality and Social*

Psychology 79, (2000), 238–50; and J. Chatman, J. Polzer, S. Barsade, and M. Neale, "Being Different Yet Feeling Similar: The Influence of Demographic Composition and Organizational Culture on Work Processes and Outcomes," *Administrative Science Quarterly* 43 (1998), 749–80.

For more on the the machinery of trust, see D. DeSteno, M. Bartlett, J. Baumann, L. Williams, and L. Dickens, "Gratitude as a Moral Sentiment: Emotion-Guided Cooperation in Economic Exchange," *Emotion* 10 (2010), 289–93; and B. von Dawans, U. Fischbacher, C. Kirschbaum, E. Fehr, and M. Heinrichs, "The Social Dimension of Stress Reactivity: Acute Stress Increases Prosocial Behavior in Humans," *Psychological Science* 23 (2012), 651–60. For a deeper exploration, see David DeSteno's *The Truth About Trust* (New York: Hudson Street, 2014).

For more on the Red Balloon Challenge, see J. Tang, M. Cebrian, N. Giacobe, H. Kim, T. Kim, and D. Wickert, "Reflecting on the DARPA Red Balloon Challenge," *Communications of the ACM* 54 (2011), 78–85; and G. Pickard, I. Rahwan, W. Pan, M. Cebrian, R. Crane, A. Madan, and A. Pentland, "Time-Critical Social Mobilization," *Science* 334 (2011), 509–12.

9 · The Super-Cooperators

For more on the origins of the Navy SEALs, see *America's First Frogman* by Elizabeth Kauffman (Annapolis, MD: Naval Institute Press, 2004). For more on the Upright Citizens Brigade, see *High-Status Characters* by Brian Raftery (New York: Megawatt Press, 2013); *The Upright Citizens Brigade Comedy Improvisational Manual* by Matt Besser, Ian Roberts, and Matt Walsh (New York: The Comedy Council of Nicea LLC, 2013); *Yes, And* by Kelly Leonard and Tom Yorton (New York: HarperBusiness, 2015); and

The Funniest One in the Room: The Lives and Legends of Del Close by Kim Howard Johnson (Chicago: Chicago Review Press, 2008).

11 · How to Create Cooperation with Individuals

For more on Bell Labs, see David Gertner's *The Idea Factory: Bell Labs and the Great Age of American Innovation* (New York: Penguin Press, 2012). For more on IDEO, see *The Art of Innovation* by Tom Kelley (New York: Currency Doubleday, 2001) and *Change by Design* by Tom Brown (New York: HarperBusiness, 2009).

For studies on concordance, see C. Marci, J. Ham, E. Moran, and S. Orr, "Physiologic Correlates of Perceived Therapist Empathy and Social-Emotional Process During Psychotherapy," *Journal of Nervous and Mental Disease* 195 (2007),103–11; and C. Marci and S. Orr, "The Effect of Emotional Distance on Psychophysiologic Concordance and Perceived Empathy Between Patient and Interviewer," *Applied Psychophysiology and Biofeedback* 31 (2006), 115–28.

13 · Three Hundred and Eleven Words

For the starlings' system of navigation, see M. Ballerini, N. Cabibbo, R. Candelier, A. Cavagna, E. Cisbani, I. Giardina, V. Lecomte, A. Orlandi, G. Parisi, A. Procaccini, M. Viale, and V. Zdravkovic, "Interaction Ruling Animal Collective Behavior Depends on Topological Rather than Metric Distance: Evidence from a Field Study," *PNAS* 105 (2008), 1232–37.

Gabriele Oettingen's work on mental contrasting can be found in *Rethinking Positive Thinking* (New York: Current, 2014), as well as G. Oettingen, D. Mayer, A. Sevincer, E. Stephens, H. Pak, and M. Hagenah, "Mental Contrasting and Goal Commitment: The Mediating Role of Energization," *Personality and Social Psychology Bulletin* 35 *(*2009), 608–22.

For more on the Pygmalion Effect, see R. Rosenthal and L. Jacobson, "Teachers' Expectancies: Determinates of Pupils' IQ Gains," *Psychological Reports* 19 (1966), 115–18. For more on how narratives affect motivation, see A. Grant, E. Campbell, G. Chen, K. Cottone, D. Lapedis, and K. Lee, "Impact and the Art of Motivation Maintenance: The Effects of Contact with Beneficiaries on Persistence Behavior," *Organizational Behavior and Human Decision Processes* 103 (2007), 53–67.

14 · The Hooligans and the Surgeons

See C. Stott, O. Adang, A. Livingstone, and M. Schreiber, "Tackling Football Hooliganism: A Quantitative Study of Public Order, Policing and Crowd Psychology," *Psychology Public Policy and Law* 53 (2008), 115–41; C. Stott and S. Reicher, "How Conflict Escalates: The Inter-Group Dynamics of Collective Football Crowd 'Violence,'" *Sociology* 32, (1998), 353–77; A. Edmondson, R. Bohmer, and G. Pisano, "Speeding Up Team Learning," *Harvard Business Review* 79, no. 9 (2001), 125–32; and A. Edmondson, R. Bohmer, and G. Pisano, "Disrupted Routines: Team Learning and New Technology Implementation in Hospitals," *Administrative Science Quarterly* 46 (2001), 685–716.

15 · How to Lead for Proficiency

See S. Reilly Salgado and W. Starbuck, "Fine Restaurants: Creating Inimitable Advantages in a Competitive Industry," doctoral dissertation, New York University Graduate School of Business Administration (2003).

16 · How to Lead for Creativity

See *Creativity Inc.* by Ed Catmull with Amy Wallace (New York: Random House, 2014).

Recommended Reading

Laszlo Bock, *Work Rules* (New York: Grand Central Publishing, 2015)

David Brooks, *The Social Animal* (New York: Random House, 2011)

Arie de Geus, *The Living Company* (Boston, MA: Harvard Business Review Press, 2002)

Angela Duckworth, *Grit: The Power of Perseverance and Passion* (New York: Scribner, 2016)

Charles Duhigg, *The Power of Habit: Why We Do What We Do in Life and Business* (New York: Random House, 2012)

Amy Edmondson, *Teaming: How Organizations Learn, Innovate, and Compete in the Knowledge Economy* (San Francisco: Jossey-Bass Pfeiffer, 2012)

Adam Grant, *Give and Take* (New York: Viking, 2013)

Richard Hackman, *Leading Teams* (Boston, MA: Harvard Business Review Press, 2002)

Chip and Dan Heath, *Switch: How to Change Things When Change is Hard* (New York: Broadway Books, 2010)

Sebastian Junger, *Tribe: On Homecoming and Belonging* (New York: HarperCollins, 2016)

James Kerr, *Legacy* (London: Constable & Robinson, 2013)

Patrick Lencioni, *The Five Dysfunctions of a Team: A Leadership Fable* (San Francisco: Jossey-Bass, 2002)

Stanley McChrystal, *Team of Teams: New Rules of Engagement for a Complex World* (New York: Portfolio, 2015).

Mark Pagel, *Wired for Culture* (New York: W. W. Norton & Company, 2012)

Daniel Pink, *Drive: The Surprising Truth About What Motivates Us* (New York: Riverhead Books, 2009)

Amanda Ripley, *The Smartest Kids in the World: And How They Got That Way* (New York: Simon & Schuster, 2013)

Edgar H. Schein, *Helping* (Oakland, CA: Berrett-Koehler Publishers, 2009)

Edgar H. Schein, *Humble Inquiry* (Oakland, CA: Berrett-Koehler Publishers, 2013)

Peter M. Senge, *The Fifth Discipline* (New York: Doubleday Business, 1990)

Michael Tomasello, *Why We Cooperate* (Cambridge, MA: MIT Press, 2009)

Upright Citizens Brigade and, 128

Felps, Will, 3–6, 74, 75

Ferguson, John, 35–36

Finding Nemo (film), 221

Fischer, Peter, 23n

Fitch, Denny, 93–95, 105

Flight 232 crash, 91–97, 254n

Folds, Jay, 42–43

Folkman, Joseph, 162

Freeman, Tom (pseudonym), 120, 120n, 122

French, Sir John, 30

Frozen (film), 216, 219, 226

future, shared with group, 11, 26, 44–45, 46
  brain function and, 39
  narrative or story and, 182
  purpose and, 182, 186–87, 198–99
  sneak-previewing of, 77–78

Gino, Francesco, 37, 79–80

Ginobili, Manu, 59

Givechi, Roshi, 149–54, 157, 163
  question modules by, 152–53
  "a scaffold of thoughtfulness" and, 163–64
  "surfacing" and, 150, 150n, 163

Give-Some Game, 106–7

Goldberg, Amir, 77n

Google, xviii, 16–21, 21n, 26

AdWords development, 16–20, 39, 250n
  belonging and, 17, 20, 26, 39
  collision opportunities at, 17
  family-esque identifiers at, 7n
  Friday forums, 17, 20
  hockey games, 17, 20
  People Analytics, 159
  X, 221n

Gortat, Marcin, 49

Gramercy Tavern, 100–101, 158, 202, 205–6

Grant, Adam, 79–80, 186–87

gratitude, 78–81, 253n, 255n
  Grant and Gino study, 79–80

Green, Danny, 50

Gross, Bill, 16

group chemistry, 8–15, 69–70

group culture, xv–xx, xvi n, 6–8, 7n, 15. *See also* purpose; safety; vulnerability
  author's selections for study, xix, xixn
  bad apple experiment, 3–6
  belonging and, 10–15, 253n
  chemistry and, 8–9, 12, 69–70
  factors in successful performance, xv–xviii, xix, 13, 14–15, 17–21, 21n, 55, 66, 69–72, 74–88, 97, 113, 158–68, 180, 186–87, 227–35
  factors which don't contribute to success, xix, 6, 15, 20–21

About the Author

DANIEL COYLE is the *New York Times* bestselling author of *The Talent Code, The Little Book of Talent, The Secret Race* (with Tyler Hamilton), and other books. Winner (with Hamilton) of the 2012 William Hill Sports Book of the Year Prize, he is a contributing editor for *Outside* magazine, and also works as a special advisor to the Cleveland Indians. Coyle lives in Cleveland, Ohio, during the school year and in Homer, Alaska, during the summer with his wife, Jen, and their four children.

danielcoyle.com
Twitter: @danielcoyle

About the Type

This book was set in Sabon, a typeface designed by the well-known German typographer Jan Tschichold (1902–74). Sabon's design is based upon the original letterforms of sixteenth-century French type designer Claude Garamond and was created specifically to be used for three sources: foundry type for hand composition, Linotype, and Monotype. Tschichold named his typeface for the famous Frankfurt typefounder Jacques Sabon (c. 1520–80).